SECRET WAKEFIELD

Paul L. Dawson

AMBERLEY

First published 2015

Amberley Publishing
The Hill, Stroud
Gloucestershire, GL5 4EP

www.amberley-books.com

Copyright © Paul L. Dawson, 2015

The right of Paul L. Dawson to be identified as the
Author of this work has been asserted in accordance
with the Copyrights, Designs and Patents Act 1988.

ISBN 978 1 4456 4692 3 (print)
ISBN 978 1 4456 4693 0 (ebook)

British Library Cataloguing in Publication Data.
A catalogue record for this book is available from the
British Library.

Typesetting by Amberley Publishing.
Printed in Great Britain.

Contents

Introduction

This book is intended to show little known aspects of the history of the city of Wakefield.

Wakefield Cathedral, interior *c.* 1880

The cathedral stands on the site of a Saxon church being replaced by a Norman church soon after 1090. Before the sixteenth century it was known as All Hallows and subsequently as All Saints. The main part of the present building is in the Perpendicular style of the early fifteenth century and was restored between 1858 and 1874 by Sir George Gilbert Scott in ashlar sandstone. The large four-stage west tower and spire are the highest in Yorkshire. Most of the cathedral's stained glass windows were created by Charles Eamer Kempe (1837–1907). The church became a cathedral in 1888 when the Diocese of Wakefield was created, although it also remained as the parish church. The chancel was extended in 1905, adding transepts and St Mark's chapel. Cathedral Passage leads from the western end of the cathedral through to Westmorland Street and still retains its railings from the 1840s. In the 1980s, a Chapter House known asTracey Hall was erected to the memory of Bishop Tracey. The cathedral interior was stripped bared of its fine Victorian pews in 2012 and the interior modernised. The reordered interior being opened over Easter 2013.

Like many towns and cities throughout the United Kingdom, Wakefield has evolved and changed over the last 1,000 years. Wakefield had long been regarded as the capital of the West Riding of Yorkshire since the middle ages, being one of the largest population centres till the late eighteenth century.

The Kings Antiquary, John Leland records in the middle of the sixteenth century that *'al the hole profite of the towne standeth by course draperie'*. The woollen trade was an important part of the towns' economy from the time of Henry VIII if not earlier. The trade became dominated during the eighteenth century by the merchant prince families of the Heywoods, Milnes and Naylor families. In the later eighteenth century, the Holdsworth family built their fortune in the dyeing of cloth. The principal activity of the town at this period was the dressing and finishing of woollen cloth. Undyed and unfinished cloths were sent to Wakefield to be dyed and finished before being dispatched to London or the continent. By 1752, Wakefield was noted for the making of worsted yarn, camblets and stuffs (a type of worsted cloth), tammy being a type of stuff. A cloth hall specialising in white cloths was opened in in 1710, and in 1778, a Tammy Hall (or Piece Hall) was opened for the sale of tammies, white cloths and blanketing. The Tammy Hall was closed sometime after 1823 when it was let to a wool stapler H. W. Wood, who converted the building into a stuff mill in 1829. In 1830, it was sold as worsted manufactory for Messrs Marriott. It was they who in 1822–23 had constructed a far larger mill on Westgate Common and a memorial to the Marriott exist in Westgate Chapel. By 1837, the Tammy Hall was occupied by James Micklethwaite, and in 1875, it was sold to Wakefield

Wakefield City Centre, 1880
The medieval layout of Wakefield with its narrow streets changed little until the years after World War II. Here we see the intensity of development between the Cathedral and Town Hall, the latter vantage point from which this image was taken.

Corporation. Following partial demolition to make way for the town hall, The Tammy Hall became part of the constabulary depot for the local police force and fire brigade and today forms part of Wakefield Magistrates court.

In addition, the economy was sustained by agriculture, principally market gardening, supplying the more densely populated towns. From the agricultural districts along the east coast, Wakefield received large quantities of corn and wool. By 1843, the corn trade in Wakefield was noted as employing

> *about three hundred vessels of from fifty to ninety tons each. The corn-market, held on Friday, is second only to that of London, and it frequently happens that for many weeks in succession the quantity sold is greater than at Mark Lane. There are ranges of large corn-warehouses on the banks of the river. Malt, which was formerly brought from other districts, is now made at Wakefield to a very large extent. The wool-fairs are also on a large scale.*

Of such importance was Wakefield's corn trade that the corn exchange and its method of sale were cited by Parliament in 1838 during the process to review and abolish the Corn

The Bull Ring *c.* 1910
Looking south towards the Parish Church from the Junction with Wood Street. Many of the Georgian buildings on the right of the image were demolished to make way for humdrum architecture.

North side of the Bull Ring *c.* 1910
Looking towards the junction with Westmoreland Street. The building in the centre of the view in 1890 was occupied by James Powell & Son, Linen Drapers, alongside which was the Grocers of Miss Mary A. Crowther and the linen Warhouse of William H. Kingswell.

Laws. By 1890, the city had a proliferation of malt houses, many built in the narrow yards running from the principle streets, or were vast complexes built along the banks of the river Calder, where between Wakefield Bridge south and Belle Isle, no fewer than sixteen malthouses and/or malthouses with kilns could be found, some being connected by both a low level Kirkigate Station Corn Warehouse belonging to the Lancashire and Yorkshire Railway and also to water transport at Thornes Wharf. Here too were three corn mills. For the sale of corn, a corn exchange was built on Westgate in 1820. It was replaced by a far larger building that stood opposite at the top of Westgate in 1837.

The Old Corn Exchange *c.* 1910

The first corn markets were held open until 1820, when Thomas Rishworth, junior partner in the bank of Wentworth, Chaloner and Rishworth, opened the first building for Wakefield corn factors. However, when the bank failed in 1825, the corn exchange was seized by the banks creditors. The building in later years became the premises of the Yorkshire Penny Bank and was demolished when the bank constructed new premises on the site in the 1930s.

In addition, the town was nationally important for its cattle market which had been established in 1765. Such was the scale of the business that by 1860 the cattle market was said to be the largest in the North of England and perhaps Europe. The cattle market closed in 1960s, but its legacy lives on with the road name 'Fair Ground Road'. Such was the scale of the undertaking for the sale of cattle that it seems that any land suitable for grazing to fatten up the cows after been walked over long distance to the market in the immediate environs of the town were turned over for this, to fatten up the cattle before sale in the market. This raised the price of the land to such a premium, which made industrial development uneconomical.

The New Corn Exchange, Photographed in 1885

At the top of Westgate, stood one of Wakefield's grandest and most important buildings, the Wakefield corn exchange and public buildings. Designed by W. L. Moffat of Doncaster, and was opened in 1838, enlarged in 1864. The corn trade in Wakefield can be dated back to the 1630s, when the first corn market was held in booths set up on Westgate. Due to water transportation, the market grew in size and importance. The inconvenience of the open air market led in 1820 to the first corn exchange being opened. This venture failed and a new company was formed in 1836, 'The Wakefield Exchange Company', to erect a larger and more imposing building. To build the new exchange, a plot of land covering 2,000 square feet at the corner of Queen Street and Westgate was purchased. The shops and houses on the site were demolished and construction commenced soon after 10th March 1837. The foundation stone was laid on 24 May 1837, with a celebratory meal being held at the neighbouring Great Bull Hotel. The 1864 enlargement created the grand saloon which was used for concerts, balls and for a while a place of worship while West Parade Wesleyan Methodist Chapel was being renovated in 1881. From 1911, the Grand Saloon became the Grand Electric Cinema and the corn market itself was converted into a Billiards Hall. The Grand Electric Cinema closed in 1959. The building was demolished in 1962 after a small fire damaged the parts of the building. This robbed Wakefield of one of its finest buildings.

The Cattle Market

The cattle market was opened in 1765 on gently sloping ground on the Ings. The land was formerly owned by the Revd Henry Zouch, the Vicar of Sandal. The loaned was let by the Wakefield Charities on 16th February 1765 on a twenty-one year lease to six persons, who agreed to enclose the land, to provide a goodly number of sheep pens and to keep the ground and road in good repair, all to be left in good repair at the end of their tenure of lease. The first market was held on 7 March 1765. The intersection of the Denby Dale Turnpike and the Ings to Kirkgate Turnpike from 1731 gave the market increased facilities for bringing cattle into for sale from surrounding grazing land. The cattle market was expanded by 2 acres in 1827. The market was held fortnightly and became a weekly market from 7 March 1849 at the request of the farmers and butchers who traded at the market. In 1805, 5,527 cattle and 100,626 sheep were sold which by 1835 had risen to 15,519 cattle and 258,780 sheep. In 1868, the sale of sheep peaked at 360,112. The same year, a pig market was established on the east of the Denby Dale Road at the end of South Parade. In 1901, 73,465 cattle, 190,662 sheep and 5,145 pigs were sold. In June 1938, the governors of the Wakefield Charities sold the cattle market to Wakefield Corporation. The market was closed in 1963 and the site became a timber yard for Drake & Warters Ltd. Upon the failure of that company in the late 1970s, the site was developed as the Royal Mail sorting office.

Wakefield was granted a market in the rein of King John. It met originally in the market place at the head of Westgate, which eventually became infilled with buildings. A market cross was erected in 1701. In the 1850s a new market was built off Westmorland Street.

The Market Cross and Cross Square *c.* 1860

At some time in the seventeenth century, the memorial cross that had been set up by Edward IV to commemorate the death of his brother Edmund Earl of Rutland was moved from Kirkgate to a site on Westgate. The cross survived the Civil War and was still standing in 1684. In approximately 1700, the inhabitants of the town complained that the market place had become so infilled with permanent shops rather than temporary booths that no convenient place existed for the sale of butter, eggs, poultry, etc. In 1707, a plan was agreed to erect a market cross with chamber over, the cost being defrayed by public subscription.

The streets commissioners, constables and town overseers met in the chamber. The market cross was demolished from 19th September 1866 at the request of shopkeepers in cross square.

Cross Square, *c.* 1910

The buildings in the centre of the view were demolished in the years prior to the First World War to widen road access to the Bull Ring.

Cross Square, *c.* 1925

Cross Square around 1925. A view that is recognisable by many people in Wakefield today.

Wakefield Borough Market

The Wakefield Borough Market Company was incorporated in 1847, on land that formerly belong to the Rectory Manor Estate. The company was not floated, however, until 30th September 1852. The company was then incorporated by statute with a capitol of £12,000 vested in its directors. The Borough Market was constructed from 1853 along with the Borough Market Hotel. The Borough Market building was erected in 1865. When the new Market Hall was built, new streets were laid out named after the directors of the company; Goodybower on which the Old Grammar School was built, became Brook Street after William Brook Naylor; Teall Street was built to connect Kirkgate and Jacobs Well Lane, named after William Teall; Parsonflatte was widened and named Westmoreland Street after M. J. R. Westmoreland who floated the company in 1852; Lady Lane became Vicarage Street and Saville Street was extended to meet Teall Street. Also laid out and named after a director of the company was Frederick Street. By the early 1900s, the twenty-eight indoor stalls sold meat, sweets, hats, ironmongery, butter, eggs and books. Outside you could buy flowers, fruit, potatoes, vegetables, fish, underwear, hats, haberdashery, tobacco, china, cloth and tripe or visit the blacksmith or the herbalist. The corporation purchased the market in 1901 for £72,584. Today, the old Victorian Market Hall and its 1960s replacement building have been demolished to make way for Trinity Walk Shopping Centre.

Looking West up Warrengate *c.* 1880

Wakefield also played its part in the development of the race horse. In 1679, races were held in the county town of the West Riding of Yorkshire, Wakefield, and in 1682, races were held between 15 and 17 August. Races differed from those of today, as races were in several heats, up to 5 miles long, and comprised at least three heats. The races were open initially in Wakefield at least to Hunters and Yorkshire Galloways. In 1711, Queen Anne had established regular race meetings at her park at Ascot. Gentlemen also organized

Looking west towards Westmoreland street and up the springs. On the right, we see the town pound as well as the 'Waver' communal horse troughs and public urinals. Beyond we see the high wall around the Vicars Croft Burial Ground.

races for themselves, often 'matching' particular horses against each other, and by 1727, a Racing Almanac began to be printed. Around 1750, the gentlemen who regularly met at the Red Lion Inn at Newmarket started the Jockey Club, and by 1791, the Jockey Club had issued the *General Stud* Book. Racing now became a fashionable and expensive sport, and new racecourses sprang up around the country. In Yorkshire, courses were established at Wetherby, Malton, York and Doncaster. Indeed, several races at Wakefield were founded by many of the great men of title in Yorkshire: Thomas Ferrand of Bingley, Cuthbert Constable of Burton Constable, William Osbaldeston of Hunmanby, Wilberforce Read of Grimethorpe, James Drummond the Duke of Duke of Perth, Lord Strafford, Earl Fitzwilliam from Wentworth Woodhouse, Vavasours from Hazelwood Castle, Sir George Armytage of Kirklees, the Kayes from Denby Grange and others of rank and patronage. By the 1770s, most race horses were thoroughbreds (TBs) thanks to the TB's greater speed, flashy action and flashy looks. The most famous TB, and perhaps the best ever bred, was of course Eclipse. By this time, the Winns of Nostell were also breeding successful race horses, thanks to the Darley Arabian, who bred most noticeably Conjecture and Bermudas. Local gentry also had their own studs, most notably Earl Fitzwilliam and the Lister Kayes, the latter owning the stallion Phenomenon, who appears in many of the pedigrees of the more successful horses of the Georgian era.

The Bull Ring *c.* 1910
With the clearing of buildings in the Market Place, the new open place became a new traffic interchange and quickly a taxi rank appeared. Here, we see the Bull Ring filled with horse cabs before the statue to Queen Victoria was installed. In later years, the Bull Ring became clogged with cars and motor vehicles.

The Statue of Queen Victoria
The statue of Queen Victoria was unveiled on 15 February 1905. Here, we see the statue before it began its many and varied migrations around the city. It moved to Thornes Park on 10th July 1950 and was moved back to the Bull in the 1980s and to Calstrop Rauxhall Square in 2012. The horse cabs have been replaced by the motor car.

Races were commonly held in Assize week, as this was when the gentry came into the chief town of the riding for trials and selling the harvest. Meets sprang up, and still run, at Newmarket in April and October, York in May, Epsom, Ascot in June, Goodwood, Doncaster, Warwick, Wakefield Malton, Manchester, Liverpool, Chester, Cheltenham, Bath, Worcester and Newcastle. Newmarket is one of horseracing's most famous historic sites, along with Malton and Middleham in Yorkshire, the true heartland of racing in this country. Although there are several instances of horse races being held in Wakefield during the seventeenth century, the main record of a Wakefield racecourse refers to the one at Outwood, where races were held from 1745 to 1794. With the enclosure act of 1793, the race course was forced to move to Pontefract. The importance of this racecourse in Wakefield can be recognised by the fact that very early on in its lifetime, sometime before 1750, the Horbury (near Wakefield) architect John Carr was commissioned to design for it a grandstand. Although better known for grand houses for the nobility of the period, during his lifetime, Carr designed several grandstands including the one, since replaced, at York racecourse, whose design is believed to have been based upon that at Wakefield. He also designed Thornes House in Wakefield and this said Westgate Chapel, also Wakefield.

At the end of the nineteenth century, Wakefield was served by excellent transport links by water, road and rail transport by water came to Wakefield under an Act of Parliament dated 4 May 1699, whereby the Aire and Calder Navigation was constructed, which opened to Wakefield from 1702. The bill was revived by Lord Fairfax, supported among others by the Magistrates of Wakefield. It was opposed by the owner of the Soke Mills at Wakefield, Francis Nevile of Chevet. The Petition read

that Leeds and Wakefield are the principal trading towns in the north for cloth; that they are situated on the Rivers Ayre and Calder, which have been viewed, and are found capable to be made navigable, which if effected, will very much redound to the preservation of the highways, and a great improvement in trade; the petitioners having no conveniency of water carriage within sixteen miles of them, which not only occasions a great expense, but many times great damage to their goods and sometimes the roads are impassable

The Grandstand of Outwood Racecourse Outwood Racecourse Grandstand around 1790, said to be designed by John Carr.

Wakefield Bridge *c.* 1880

Wakefield Bridge with the chantry chapel dates from the fourteenth century. The bridge was originally 16 feet in width and was widened in 1758 by 9 feet with the addition of nine pointed arches to the west side. A second enlargement, again of 9 feet was carried out in 1797, widening the bridge to 34 feet, allowing two-stage waggons to pass side by side as well as to leave a foot way on either side.

In 1930, Wakefield Corporation, the Aire and Calder Navigation Co. and the Ministry of Transport agreed to build a new bridge some 75 feet in width in a direct line from the bottom of Kirkgate where the road passed under the railway, alleviating the dog leg turn to the Chantry Bridge and the bottle neck caused by the narrow bridge. The new bridge was opened on 1st June 1933 and cost £50,000 to construct.

A second source of water transport, the Upper Calder Navigation linked Wakefield to other business centres from 1758 when the act was passed which authorised its construction. Later canals and navigations that linked Wakefield to wider markets were the Barnsley Canal which was built from 1793 onwards. However, the tolls from the Aire and Calder Navigation by 1730 were so small that the company was taken over by lessee.

The Aire and Calder Navigation carried more than just woollen goods. In 1830, Smithson's tramway, which conveyed coal from the mines at New Park, the Lake Lock Railroad which we note was the world's first public railway decades before the Surrey Iron Railway, the Stockton & Darlington or Liverpool & Manchester railway as well as a railroad belonging to the Duke of Leeds (Fentons Railway), transported coal to staiths on the navigation. The Lake Lock Railway and Fenton's Railway transported 110,000 to 150,000 tons of coal to the staiths on the navigation every year. Coal mining became a boom industry in the town as the nineteenth century progressed. Such was the importance of coal mining to the commerce of the city that the National Coal Board eventually became Wakefield's largest employer with Manor Colliery on Cross Lane and Park Hill Colliery at Eastmoor in operation until 1981 and 1983, respectively. Indeed, by

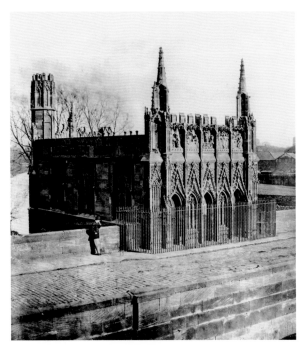

The Chantry Chapel on Wakefield Bridge

The original fourteenth century stone bridge carrying the main route to London and the South exists alongside what is now a four-lane bridge, first built in 1933. The Chantry Chapel is one of only four surviving bridge chapels in England and is a scheduled ancient monument and a Grade 1 listed building. The original stonework can be seen at the base, although much of upper part was rebuilt in 1847–48. George Gilbert Scott's west front had deteriorated so far that it had to be replaced in 1939.

the early nineteenth century, it was estimated that a seagoing vessel of one hundred tons burthen could reach Wakefield from the Humber, a journey said to take eight hours.

In the middle decades of the eighteenth century, a second transport revolution took place with the establishment of turnpike trusts in the West Riding as a whole. The promoters of these toll roads promised an alternative system of transport than offered by the canals and navigations. From 1741, Wakefield was linked to the then expanding turnpike network: linked to Halifax via the Wakefield and Weeland turnpike road, Wakefield and Halifax turnpike road and the Doncaster to Halifax road which also ran through Wakefield, and linked the town to the Great North Road, parts of which became turnpike from 1745. The first entirely new route to come directly to Wakefield was in 1789, and was the Wakefield to Aberford road, and replaced a section of the older road from Wakefield to York. The new road passed mostly across countryside where there had been no previous road. In 1825, the new Denby Dale road was authorised to be constructed by Act of Parliament and extended ultimately to Holmfirth, Stalyrbidge and Manchester. To meet the new road on the Ings, Market Street was opened up from the top of Westgate and passed along the side of the cattle market. The road was disturnpiked in 1874. A third turnpike was built, planned to link Kirkgate to Westgate bypassing the then town centre, work commencing in 1831. In 1863, the road was purchased by the Wakefield Local Board. This road today is Ings road. In the more modern era, the building of the M1 and M62 motorways connected Wakefield to a system of fast, safe and modern roads. With the turnpikes, coaching Inns flourished in Wakefield, notably the Strafford Arms and the Great Black Bull.

The Strafford Arms Hotel
The Strafford Arms Hotel, named about the Lord of the Manor, was once the principle posting house in the town. The building we see was constructed from March 1723. The Strafford Arms was demolished to make way for a more utilitarian buildings that occupy the site, one of which is named the Strafford Arms and is a public house.

The third and final transport revolution in Wakefield was the coming of the railways. The era of the stage coach and the canal was at its zenith, when a new method of locomotion was introduced, the steam engine. Following, the successful use of steam locomotives at Charles Brandlings Railway, later the Middleton Coillery Railway, Leeds by John Blenkinsop in 1812, and the Rainhill Trials of 1829, railway mania as it has been called set in. The North Midland railway was the first company which brought a line to the Wakefield area, the station being some 3 miles to the south-east at Oakenshaw. The line ran from Leeds to Derby and was opened on 30 June 1840. Joseph Hunter, a South Yorkshire Historian noted that he travelled from Oakenshaw to London in eight hours or less, recording that the time of the journey being something marvellous, as it had previously taken a couple of days to traverse the same distance. The first railway line to pass through Wakefield was the Manchester & Leeds railway, which became in later years part of Lancashire & Yorkshire Railway. The line ran from Manchester to Wakefield and then via Normanton to Leeds. George Stephenson was the engineer and commenced work in the summer of 1838, the most important engineering being the viaduct over Kirkgate and beyond, the Park Hills cutting and the bridge over the River Calder at Kirkthorpe. The construction of the line was opposed by the Aire & Calder Navigation Company, whose canal's route ran practically alongside the railway throughout a great proportion of its course. An injunction was brought by the Navigation to prevent the building of a viaduct over Kirkgate, and on 10 March 1840, the York Jury allowed for the erection of a three-arch viaduct over Kirkgate, though a single-span bridge would have been preferable. In 1900, a new single-span bridge was erected when the line to Barnsley was widened. The first Kirkgate station was opened on 5 October 1840 on the site of Aspdins Portland Cement works, which removed to Ings road until closure in 1892. The station was a small wooden hut with platform in front, with 'miserable waiting room accommodation'. A new station, the current Kirkgate station, was opened some years later in 1857.

The Great Black Bull Hotel
In the centre of the image can be seen the Great Bull Hotel. It stands on the corner of Westgate and Market Street. The current premises were erected in the 1770s and were once the foremost inns in Wakefield. Behind it was a long yard, with stabling and wool warehousing.

The next line to be constructed was by the Wakefield, Pontefract & Goole Railway. The first sod was cut on 24 September 1845 by Mr Robert Pemberton Milnes of Fryston Hall, the whole line being opened for traffic on 29 March 1848.

In 1857, the Line from Wakefield to Leeds was opened and had resulted in a portion of John Milnes Mansion on Westgate. An Act was obtained in 1862 by the West Riding and Grimsby Railway for the construction of a line from Doncaster to Wakefield, including a station in Wakefield, which was intended to be placed on the Ings. The line was built, but it was felt that the proposed new station would be inconvenient, being 40 feet above surrounding land. New plans were prepared by which it was sought to take the line through the old station on Westgate and build a new one on the north side of Westgate. A viaduct approaching the new station, consisting of ninety-five arches, nearly a mile long was built, and required 800,000,000 bricks. It is known locally as the 'ninety-nine arches', despite not numbering ninety-nine arches. An iron bridge was built to cross the Calder. The new Westgate Station was opened in 1867, with a 77-feet-high clock tower. It was swept away in the 1960s and the utilitarian building that replaced the main Italianate style station building. This too has been demolished and a new station erected on Mulberry Way.

Kirkgate Station
TThe first Kirkgate station was opened on 5 October 1840 on the site of Aspdins Portland Cemenet works, which removed to Ings road until closure in 1892. The station was a small wooden hut with platform in front, with 'miserable waiting room accommodation'.

The present station with a classical stone facade dates from 1854, built with grain warehouses adjoining it. The station after years of neglect has been magnificently restored in recent years.

Although a number of tramway schemes had been proposed for Wakefield from the 1870s onward, the first to be constructed was promoted by a group of local businessmen and authorised by the Wakefield & District Light Railway Order of 1901. On the 25 April 1903, the Yorkshire Electric Tramways Construction Syndicate Ltd was formed to build the tramway. The West Riding Tramway Act of 1904 authorised the Wakefield and District Light Railway Company to construct additional Wakefield lines together with various extensions which connected the Five Towns area with Wakefield and Leeds.

Westgate Station
Westgate Station was built in 1867, with a 77-feet-high clock tower. It was swept away in the 1960s, and the utilitarian building that replace it is too scheduled for demolition.

Horse Bus on Northgate
Horse bus outside the cathedral around 1900. These horse buses were replaced by trams and motors buses in the years either side of the First World War.

Traffic on Northgate, *c.* 1880
Horse drawn vehicles passing outside
the west door of Wakefield Cathedral.

Tram on Westgate, *c.* 1910
A tram passing down Westgate, with
the old corn exchange building in the
background.

Due to better transport links, the cloth trade flourished in Wakefield. A number of dyehouses and large worsted mills were established in the town and immediate vicinity. Vast warehouses were built below Wakefield Bridge at Navigation Yard and again from the opening of the original Fall Ing Lock beyond the junction of the new cut and the canalised river Calder. The establishment of these mills, together with the development and expansion of other industries, such as brewing, malting, rope making, mining, engineering and chemical and soap industries helped to widen the economic base of the town. It was here that James Aspdin developed and manufactured Portland cement, initially in premises upon Primrose Hill and then in a factory on Ings road. Edward Greens economiser works as well as soap works, and brick works provided other substantial contributions to the economy of the town.

The trade in corn and wool, resulted in the need for available funds in the form of hard cash by the merchants dealing with these products. For the cloth trade to function, the merchant needed cash payments, to buy cloth and pay his journeymen's wages. Therefore, the need to transmute Bills of Exchange (for example, from payments for cloth shipments) into regular supplies of cash resulted in the formation of banks in the town from the 1780s.

Trams in the Bull Ring, *c.* 1910
A tram in the Bull Ring, around 1910.

The Wakefield and Barnsley Union Bank

This magnificent building was designed by H. F. Lockwood in 1877–78 for the Wakefield and Barnsley Union Bank which moved here from its more modest premises just lower down Westgate. With the failure in 1825 Wentworth, Chaloner & Rishworth, the Huddersfield Banking Company opened an Agency in Wakefield. In 1832, the Wakefield Banking Co. was formed, becoming in 1840 the Wakefield & Banrsley Union Bank with the purchase of Beckett & Co. of Barnsley. The bank later merged with Barclay's and the building became home to the ill-fated Wakefield Building Society. In the 1970s, the shock discovery was made that the present and previous general managers had, over many years, embezzled a fortune. The Society merged immediately with the Halifax Building Society. Today the building houses a night club.

Standing hard by two doors down Westgate towards the Railway bridge is 'Bank House'. This was Wakefield's first purpose-built bank and housed the banking firm of Ingram and Kennet. This bank closed on 14th July 1814 after being in fiscal difficulties from 1808. The property was later taken over by the Wakefield and Barnsley Union Bank (established in 1832) and here from 1841, when his father became the manager, lived John Bacchus Dykes. Dykes was later ordained and became one of the most prolific composers of hymn tunes, many of which are still very well known today.

Rishworth House

Standing on Bond Street at the head of Rishworth Street stood Rishworth House. The house and garden are at the centre of the image and is surrounded by high brick wall. Rishworth House was built by Thomas Rishworth (1772–1843) for his son Thomas. Thomas Rishworth senior was appointed the first clerk at the bank of 'Ingram, Kennett Dawson and Ingram', which opened in Wakefield in 1794. In November 1802, he formed his own bank in partnership with Townend of York. This firm was known as 'Townend and Rishworth'.

Shortly after surviving a run on its resources in January 1812, the bank amalgamated with that of Wentworth and Chaloner of York and became 'Wentworth, Chaloner and Rishworth'. Thomas Rishworth's banking activities made him an extremely wealthy man. In 1826, he estimated his worth at £100,000, a fortune in those days, stating that he had but a hundred pounds to begin with. This was the result of having been 'a slave for 36 years'.

Thomas and his family lived in Birthwaite Hall, near Darton, and were apparently pillars of the Wakefield community. He built Rishworth house in Bond Street, Wakefield, for his son Thomas, who was also a partner in the bank. In 1805, Thomas senior was the Chief Constable of Wakefield, forerunner of the office of mayor. He also served on the Poor Relief and Watch Committees and was elected Governor of the Wakefield Grammar School.

However, the family fortunes suffered a severe reversal following the collapse of the bank in December 1825, an event from which the economic health of Wakefield took years to recover. Thomas was declared bankrupt the next year and was forced to sell Birthwaite Hall and his extensive library of rare books. Rishworth was occupied by Todd Naylor after its sale. The Naylors are recalled by Henry Clarkson in his memories of *Merry Wakefield.*

For Wakefield, the thirty-year period from 1785 witnessed a huge expansion of business, primarily in the cloth trade. The receipts of the Leeds to Halifax turnpike rose from £852 to £3,500 between 1785 and 1800, and the receipts for the Aire and Calder Navigation tolls trebled from £40,033 a year in 1782 to £150,268 in 1802. This rapid growth being brought about by the growth of the Southern American markets, the Home market which also included the supply of broadcloth to the Army and Navy. From 1806, the Continental System which banned the sale of English goods in Europe helped also to swell the Home market. However, few of these merchant princes in Wakefield became manufacturers, and some like the Naylors had no desire to copy the model established in Halifax of merchant manufacturers, and understood the role of merchant and manufacturer being quite separate: the merchant finished the cloth through fulling, dyeing and dressing and did not make the cloth, the cloth being supplied from often smaller concerns.

Bond Street, *c.* 1880
The high walls around Rishworth House and properties on the eastern side of Bond Street dominate this view, of what was in 1880, a residential area with a semi-rural feel.

Sat John's Square, *c.* 1880
This Georgian development, promoted by John
Lee, a Wakefield solicitor, was completed soon
after 1800, with a uniform frontage design, but
irregular backs. Some were built as shells – just
walls, roofs and floors; interior dividing walls were
added later.

St John's North, *c.* 1880
The house at the eastern end, and seven other houses were erected by a building society, 'The Union
Society' led by John Puckrin a local builder. Like St John's Square, they were all constructed with a
uniform design for the frontage by John Thompson, an eminent architect. This has survived almost
intact, apart from an altered doorway and the addition of an oriel window.

As well as the trade in broad cloths, there was a strong manufacturing presence of worsted yarns and cloths like shalloons and serges. By 1835, there were ten steam powered worsted mills and one water power mill employing 1,028 staff; by 1838, this had risen to thirteen steam powered mills of 240 horse power employing 916 per mill and in 1850, there were seventeen mills, with 34,167 spindles and 1,195 staff. In addition was a single mill, both spinning and weaving cloth with 480 spindles and 163 looms employing fourteen men and 168 women. The concerns of Marriott and Barker (later Paten and Baldwin) became important business in the town.

By 1810, fuelled by this peak in commerce, Wakefield gained many new civic institutions. The leading townsfolk had established a number of educational establishments and both voluntary and philanthropic organisations, of which number was a library founded in 1786 and the Dispensary founded in 1787. From 1803, there appeared the '*Wakefield Star and West Riding Advertiser*'. New assembly rooms were built and opened in Crown Court, and further civic developments witnessed the foundation of the Music Saloon in the newly laid out Wood Street. Indeed, Wakefield was considered to be in many civil matters, the capital of the West Riding, as it had many institutions which were used by the whole region: a prison, the office of the Clerk of the Peace, a Registry of Deeds, the principal court of the election of Members of Parliament of the West Riding, as well as the county lunatic asylum.

Pemberton House
Pemberton House, at the entrance to Westgate Station, is one of the many fine and large Georgian houses on both sides of Westgate, most of which still exist; a reminder of the many successful merchants that prospered in Wakefield during the eighteenth century. An American visitor in 1777 stated that 'Westgate Street has the most noble appearance I ever saw out of London'. Pemberton House was built in about 1752 for Pemberton Milnes. The Milnes family were successful cloth and wine merchants, and various branches of the family owned houses on Westgate. Pemberton Milnes became a magistrate and a Deputy Lieutenant of Yorkshire; he was a Whig and a dissenter, supporting the Westgate Chapel where he would eventually be buried in the vaults.

County Court
Land was purchased in 1806, and the Court House built for the West Riding magistrates to a design provided by Charles Watson, an architect based in Doncaster and who was also an architect of the St Johns and South Parade developments and West Parade Wesleyan Chapel. A delay in completion was reputed to be because there were problems obtaining large enough blocks of stone for the pillars, but Quarter Sessions were held there from 1810. The building was extended in 1849–50 and again in the 1880s. County Courts ceased to be held there in 1992, and at present, the building remains empty.

Economic instability from 1826 saw the collapse of a Wakefield based bank and heralded a period of gradual decline. One of the most serious aspects of this decline was the stagnation of some fields of the cloth industry, which had an adverse effect on the economy of the town, paralleled in the economic activity of the community, its cultural and social life and other institutions.

The social structure of the Wakefield, like other nearby towns, contained a large 'middle class' which constituted business men, lawyers, agents, bankers, accountants and members of the medical profession, reflecting the towns function as a service centre and market. In 1851, 7 per cent of the population could be classed as 'professional', 21 per cent as intermediate, employing up to twenty-five workers. The remainder were working class. The register of electors also reflects the stability of the middle class in Wakefield; in 1832, 5.9 per cent of the population were qualified to vote, which by 1865 was 6.1 per cent. Local towns like Bradford and Leeds were growing faster due to an increase in the working-class sector, as workers followed work, while Wakefield attracted both middle and working-class families. Despite a slower population growth, than experienced by

Theatre Royal, Drury Lane
James Banks, in 1776, built Wakefield's first purpose-built theatre, the Theatre Royal on Westgate. Many famous actors starred there, including Mrs Siddons and Edmund Kean. It was managed by Tate Wilkinson. It was condemned as a building in 1892 and Benjamin Sherwood, the owner at that time, had it demolished. A new theatre was built in 1894, to the design of the well-known theatre architect Frank Matcham, and renamed the Royal Opera House.

Leeds for example, between 1801 and 1851, the population of Wakefield increased by over 50 per cent. However, growth in population was not uniform throughout the North. Centres of manufacture and ports rapidly increased in populous while Market Towns, and other settlements, in certain instances become depopulated.

Westgate, looking towards the Cathedral
Shops on the northside of Westgate around 1910.

Premises of James Brown, Brass Founders, Providence Yard
Buildings on Providence Yard, Kirkgate. In the many small yards, houses stood
shoulder to shoulder with factories and warehouses.

Office of James Brown, Brass Founders

Interior of an officer on Providence Yard Kirkgate, in the 1930s.

Terrace houses on Rishworth Street

Population growth in the eighteenth century and early years of the nineteenth century manifested itself with extensive and unrestricted building of small houses on every available piece of land, including the centres of some wide streets and yards dating back to the medieval origins of the town. Down the side of the yards were built rows of small houses, leaving narrow passage ways either side, 3 to 4 feet in width. The west side of Kirkgate was a typical example of this type of building, a wide main street with some fashionable houses fronting the street with at intervals, passageways leading to dark alleys running at right angles between the houses. Water was supplied from wells. Ranger notes in his report that in the towns 168 lanes, yards and streets examined in 1847, ventilation of twenty-two were good, being open at both ends, thirty-one middling, open at one end, and 115 bad, being totally enclosed. In these 168 lanes, there was a population of 13,074 living in 2,707 houses. Of these houses only eigh yards and courts had good drainage, sixteen 'middling', and 144 bad that is that the street acted as a gutter. Thus, over 70 per cent of the population of Wakefield in 1847 were living in badly ventilated, badly lighted, badly built and badly drained houses.

Westgate, *c.* 1880
Looking West down Westgate. The scene has changed since 1885 with the addition of the Unity Hall, the Theatre Royal & Opera House premises of 1894 and the Picture House of 1913, all three grand buildings adding an air of dignity to Upper Westgate. Also a notable change was the demolition of the Wool Hall where wool cloth was sold and its replacement by the attractive premises of HSBC Bank in the 1920s.

North side of Silver Street, *c.* 1880
View of the buildings on the south side of Silver Street at the junction with Mary Gate. The building to the left of the image was in 1890 the Grocers establishment of John Macguir & Co. Next door stood the Shades Public House, the landlord in 1890 being John W. Brown.

This narrow street linked cross square to the head of Westgate. Existing streets in the town centre once bounded the medieval market and village green: the top of Westgate, Silver Street, Little Westgate, Bull Ring and the section of Northgate outside the Cathedral gates. Buildings abutting on Bread Street and Cross Square developed from medieval booths to become permanent shops. Silver Street was formerly the Leather Booths.

Silver Street from the West, *c.* 1910

Looking up Silver Street towards cross square around 1910. On the left, we see the entrance to King Street. The large four-storey warehouse on King Street, which is entered off Silver Street was built for Joseph Jackson about 1811. Here he took Titus Salt as his apprentice to learn the wool trade, later to become the builder of Salts Mill and Saltaire. Entered from King Street is Barstow Square and was named after the Barstow family who purchased the Green Dragon Inn in 1708, the square is typical of the infilling and rebuilding that happened elsewhere in the town from the early eighteenth century onwards.

West of Barstow Square, entered from King Street, Thompson's Yard is typical of the many yards that once existed in Wakefield, leading off from the three main thoroughfares, Northgate, Westgate and Kirkgate. They were originally paved with cobbles (later replaced with setts), which were often brought in by boat on the navigation. George Gissing (1857–1903), the renowned Victorian novelist, lived here as a boy behind his father's chemist's shop. Although he left Wakefield as a young man, his early experiences in Wakefield are often reflected in his writing. He wrote twenty-three novels, short stories and two studies of Charles Dickens

One of the worst areas of the town was around Nelson Street, where the inhabitants were mainly of Irish extraction, having migrated to the town during the building of the railway and canals. The 1851 census reveals that in the 26 dwellings in Nelson Street had a population of 233 persons, an average of nine persons per dwelling, whereas on average, five people occupied each dwelling in the town. This means that Nelson Street and surrounding area had a population 125 per cent higher than the overall average for the town. This average is however misleading, as a number of houses had less than average occupancy and some more: six houses were occupied by four or less, and others between six and sixteen. In general, the houses in the town with the highest occupancy rates were those in which the householder or his wife's occupation was noted as being 'Lodging House Keeper'. Indeed, it was not until the 1871 Public Health Act that back-to-back houses were prohibited. However, while this regulation applied to the building of working-class houses, the houses of the middle and upper classes had been subject to regulations regarding sewage disposal, ventilation, paving and design as early as 1800 but not by statute.

Premises of the Bank of Leathem Tew & Co.
The building on the right in our day Barclays Bank was built by the concern of Leathem, Tew & Co. The concern began in 1801 in Pontefract. The Wakefield branch was established in 1808 what had been a drapery establishment of Mr Timothy Hick that stood on the same site. The current building was erected in 1881 in 'Queen Anne' style of architecture. In this view of Silver Street taken around 1880, we catch a glimpse of The Black Swan building on Silver Street, with its stepped upper levels, is of seventeenth century origin, dating from a time when timber was still the basic structural material.

Wakefield City Centre, *c.* 1880
Looking to the Town Hall from the Cathedral Tower. The density of buildings in the city centre is very evident in this image.

The 1871 Act also gave the Corporation the power to close houses unfit for human inhabitation but does not appear to have been applied in Wakefield. Prior to the act being passed, new residential areas, of back-to-back housing were constructed throughout the town and neighbourhood. New streets were laid out and houses built between Northgate and Stanley Road; Saville Street, York Street, etc., being examples. This area was gradually in filled, the new working-class housing contrasting starkly with the early Victorian middle-class houses on College Grove Road and the development of large Victorian villas around Westfield. Other developments occurred off Westgate, New Scarborough and New Brighton being laid out at this time as was Belle Vue and Primrose Hill.

Looking towards St John's, *c.* 1950

Looking from the Cathedral Tower north towards St John's. The yards packed into the area between Northgate and Wood Street have all most been cleared away.

Cottages on Marygate *c.* 1880

Mary Gate in the middle ages was the site of the Manor of Wakefield Bake House. It was here that all those desiring to bake bread or bake pies and pastries had to come and have these items baked. Also here was the town gaol, after which the street was named 'Prison Lane'.

In the photograph, we see this row of charming sixteenth century cottages. They were demolished in 1901 for a road widening scheme. The brick building to the right of the image stood on the end of the row before it was demolished. This building in 1890 was the premises of a Straw Hat Maker and by 1901 a Sewing Machine Factory.

The population of Wakefield grew by just over 50 per cent between 1801 and 1850 and manifested itself with extensive and unrestricted building of small houses on every available piece of land, including along the edges of yards dating back to the medieval origins of the town. To cater for the population boom, new streets were laid out and houses built between Northgate and Stanley Road; Saville Street, York Street, etc., being examples. This area was gradually in filled, the new working-class housing contrasting starkly with the early Victorian middle-class houses on College Grove Road and the development of large Victorian villas around Westfield. Other developments occurred off Westgate, New Scarborough and New Brighton being laid out at this time as was Belle Vue and Primrose Hill. In the years immediately after the First World War, new council housing schemes were constructed, the first being at Portobello in Belle Vue, constructed from 1924, to replace the cramped and often over crowded inner city housing stock. New council estates were built in Lupset (from 1921), Eastmoor and Darnley (from 1930) and at Flanshaw and Peacock (from 1936). Lupset estate was expanded in the 1960s with the building of houses at Snapethorpe. As well as provision for new working-class homes, between Dewsbury and Alverthorpe Road, a new 'Garden City' housing scheme

The Black Rock Public House and Cross Square, *c.* 1880
The late eighteenth century Black Rock public house is on the site of the house where John Potter lived as a child. He was to be Archbishop of Canterbury from January 1737 until his death in 1747. The landlord of which in 1890 was John W. Allen. The pub stands hard by a triple gabled late medieval house that was demolished around 1900.

was developed for the more affluent members of the working. Ribbon development also occurred in the 1920s and 1930s along Horbury road and Thornes road as the city expanded and developed new suburbs. High rise living came to Wakefield in the 1950s and 1960s, the tower blocks dotted around Wakefield dominate the skyline. In more recent times, new private housing schemes have been built both on outlying land around Wakefield on or derelict industrial sites close to the Waterfront or by Westgate Railway Station. Mills and warehouses on the waterfront and former Methodist Chapels have also been converted into private accommodation

Kirkgate, *c.* 1880
The buildings on the east side of Kirkgate as they appeared in 1880. Today virtually nothing from this photograph can be identified in the modern street scape.

Kirkgate, *c.* 1880
The west side of Kirkgate as it was around 1880.

West side of Kirkgate,
photographed between Grove
Road and Charlotte Street, *c.* 1880
West side between Grove road and
Charlotte Street on the west side
of Kirkgate could be found in 1888,
on the corner of Grove Road and
Kirkgate John Willam Furness, Book
Seller & Stationer, at Nos 171 and
173 Kirkgate was Webster Brothers
Grocers, whose sign we can see
hanging above the foot path, then
the premises of Ms Sarah Driver
earthenware dealer, Thomas Henry
Raper, Ironmonger and thence the
Spotted Leopard Public House,
the publican being Robert Henry
Broadhead. The premises on the
extreme left of the image were those
of William Sanderson printer and
bookseller.

East side of Kirkgate
photographed between Grove
Road and Charlotte Street,
c. 1880
East Side. Here we see the buildings
that stood betwixt the junction
of Kirkgate and Park Street and
the junction of Kirkgate and
William Street. The junction with
William Street is behind the horse and
cart in the centre of the image. The
building partial obscured by the horse
and cart was in 1888 the premises of
Mrs Eliza Thornton, Confectioner
and those of James Ellis & Sons Boot
Makers. Over the street stood at 178
Kirkgate the premises of Benjamin
Sherwood Provisions Merchant, at 180
and 188 Kirkgate were William Edward
Wilman Fruitier, and Lister Rawson,
Clothier. At 192 and 194 Kirkgate was
William Kendall tailor and Hatter,
at 192 and 194 Kirkgate John Ogden
Milliner, and thence out of shot was
William and John Simpson, Bakers.

The responsibility for the government of Wakefield lay with the board of 161 Commissioners, who were nominated under the Improvement Act of 1771, who were responsible for the state of the streets, sewerage and drainage. However, by the 1840s, there was dissatisfaction with the Commissioners' application of their powers, and a committee was formed to apply for a charter of Incorporation.

The Moot Hall

In the middle ages, governance of the town was vested with the steward of the Lord of the Manor. In terms of legal governance, the manor court was held in the Moot Hall, moot being an old English word meaning an assembly. This building stood close to the parish church, on Kirkgate in Manor House Yard along with the Rolls Office. There was little furniture other than a rough table and a bench, which were for the lord's officers. Everyone else had to stand. The steward of the Earl of Warrenne presided over the court. There was also a criminal court known as the Tourn.

Wakefield received its charter of incorporation in 1848 and was to consist of twenty-four elected councillors and eight aldermen. The first election took place on 13 May 1848, and George William Harrison, at some time both a Quaker and Methodist, became the first mayor. The charter allowed for the government of the new borough (not to be confused with the medieval borough), to be undertaken by two bodies: the corporation and the commissioners, who were responsible for the paving, street lighting, sewers and cleansing, while the corporation was responsible for the police and fire service. Dissatisfaction with the commissioners' inability to improve the conditions of the town lead to a public meeting of the leading citizens to request that the Public Health Act of 1848 be applied to Wakefield. As a result of a report made by William Ranger a civil servant, a Board of Health was constituted in 1852 to undertake improvements to the sanitary condition of the town.

The administrative centre of the County Council of the West Riding was established in Wakefield in 1889 through the Local Government Act 1888. This came to an end in 1974 when the West Yorkshire Metropolitan County Council was formed. County Hall was built to accommodate the County Council in the four years from 1894, being officially opened by the Marquess of Ripon on 22 February 1898. The original building was extended within a few years, with new wings being added between 1912 and 1915. The builder was George Crook of Wakefield. The council was discontinued in 1986, and the county hall was acquired by the city of Wakefield Metropolitan District Council in December 1987 to continue the use of the building for local government purposes – as the council's main headquarters. The governance of Wakefield from 1848 was vested in the town council, which met at first in a building in Crown Court before the current town hall was built.

County Hall, *c.* 1905
The West Riding County Council was established in 1889. In 1892, architects' designs were invited for its headquarters. The winning design was by Gibson and Russell who proposed a Gothic design. County Hall was built in the four years from 1894 and opened by the Chairman of the West Riding County Council, Charles George Milnes Gaskell, on 22 February 1898. New wings were added to the original building between 1912 and 1915 by George Crook of Wakefield. The interior of the building is embellished by splendid mural paintings, tiling and mosaic.

At the end of the nineteenth century, medical treatment was provided for the poor people of Wakefield by medical charities along with an increasing number of private doctors and medical men. Wakefield in the middle decades of the twentieth century could boast five hospitals as well as the West Riding Lunatic Asylum, originating from the first half of the nineteenth century or earlier. Clayton Hospital moved from Wood Street to Northgate between 1876 and 1879 with the construction of new buildings. The infirmary of the New Union Workhouse on Park Lodge Lane (erected 1851) was developed as Wakefield County Hospital, becoming part of the National Health Service in 1948. After 1968, it too catered mainly for elderly patients. All the workhouse buildings have now been demolished and the site is occupied by a housing estate.

Pinderfield's General Hospital originated as part of the West Riding Pauper Lunatic Asylum (established 1818) through the efforts of Dr William Bevan Lewis in 1867 to provide separate accommodation for the recently diagnosed mentally ill. The Hospital was expanded in 1899, with new buildings being opened on 8 March 1900, at a total cost of £69,000. However, outbreak of war in September 1939 designated the hospital as an emergency hospital to treat the war injured. Farmland next to the hospital was acquired and wooed huts were built to increase capacity. The mental patients were transferred to asylums across West Riding. Today a new Pinderfields General Hospital has replaced the former premises. Clayton Hospital, Pinderfields Hospital and the County Hospital in 1948 provided state funded healthcare under the terms of the Beveridge report. Snapethorpe Isolation Hospital was constructed and opened in 1907 and closed in 1959. Maternity cover was provided from 1931 by Manygates hospital as well as private midwives.

Education in Wakefield at the turn of the nineteenth century was provided by a number of different bodies. Charitable schools comprised the Queen Elizabeth Grammar School and the Greencoat School. The established church provided parish schools such as the Bell School, Lancasterian School and Holy Trinity School's. The Wesleyan Methodist Church rang the Methodist Day School. Private schools also existed, one such being the Heath Academy. Through the Education act of 1870 the Board Schools on Ings road, Westgate and Eastmoor road were built (at some intervals). Attendance at school from the ages of four to twelve was compulsory by Act of Parliament in 1880. As the twentieth century

Wakefield Gaol
Governor's Mansion of Wakefield Gaol. The town gaol on the Middle Ages was in Mary Gate. The current site off Back Lane was taken up in the mid-sixteenth century. The prison has been rebuilt many times since then.

progressed, empowered by the 1948 education act, more schools were built and others moved to new buildings, such as Thornes House School, and the Cathedral School moving from the Old grammar School on Brooke Street to new premises on Thornes road.

The Bell School

The Bell School on Bell Street was built in 1813. It was built by supporters of the Revd Andrew Bell who formed in 1811 'The National Society for promoting education of the Poor in the Principles of the National Church'. The Revd Andrew Bell was the son of a barber who traded in St Andrews. While serving as an Army chaplain in India he devised his own method of education. His system of education was applied the Protestant Charity School at Aldgate London in 1798. Bell's supporters desired to bring the education of the poor under the influence of the Church of England, with schools under the direct control of parochial clergy. Joseph Lancaster a support of Bells principles and his supporters favoured a Christian education on none sectarian lines. The Bell School was opened in 1813 for boys and in 1818 a school for girls was opened on Alsmhouse Lane. When the Church School in Zetland Street was built, both schools closed. The Bell Street premises became the School of Art and Craft which opened in 1868, on the back of profits made from the Wakefield Fine Art and Industrial Exhibition of August 1865. This school had been founded in 1841 and was based at the Music Saloon Wood Street from 1855. A technical school was opened on 30th April 1891. From 3 April 1900, the college was handed over to Wakefield Corporation. New buildings were erected in 1929, 1933, 1941, 1962 and 2012. These buildings contribute to the city scape of Wakefield and form a visual terminus to the line of sight along wood street.

Queen Elizabeth Grammar School, Brooke Street
The Elizabethan premises of the Grammar school which was built on Goodybower, latterly known as Brooke Street.

Rear view of the Northgate premises of Queen Elizabeth Grammar School, Wakefield.

The apparent lack of religious belief (or at least its practice) among the working class and urban poor was a constant Victorian concern. In the first half of the nineteenth century, Wakefield and area gained several new parishes, and in the town itself the parishes of Holy Trinity (20 October 1844), St Mary's Primrose Hill (3 September 1844), St Andrew on Peterson road (3 September 1844) and St Michaels (1869) were created. Wakefield had a strong sense of non-conformist worship, and by 1936, Wakefield as an area had over thirty Methodist chapels. The grandest of the Methodist Chapels was West Parade Wesleyan Chapel, opened in 1803. Market Street United Methodist Free Church of 1857, Grove Road Methodist new Connexion Chapel of 1866 and Brunswick United Methodist Free Church also of 1866 all added to the architecture of the city scape. The Unitarian Chapel on Westgate (built in 1752) had members from the great and good of the local citizenry. Indeed, Westgate Chapel and its congregation played a leading part in the social, civic and economic development of Wakefield. In later decades, the congregations at Zion Chapel and West Parade Chapel played a part in the town's economic and social development. In 1888, when the Diocese of Wakefield was formed, the parish church became Wakefield Cathedral and the town became a city. William Walsham How was the first bishop.

St John the Baptist's Parish Church
The foundation stone of the first new post-Reformation Anglican church in Wakefield was laid in November 1791 and the church was consecrated in 1795. Built with stone from Newmillerdam subscriptions covered part of the cost, plus the sale of pews and burial vaults.

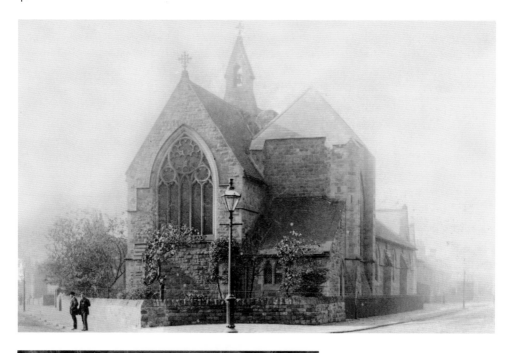

St Michaels Parish Church
St Michael's Parish church on
Westgate Common was built
in the 1860s to serve the largely
working-class area.

Brunswick Chapel
Brunswick Chapel on Saville Street was
opened in 1876. It was closed in 1985 and
demolished to make way for housing.

Eastmoor Methodist Chapel
The first Methodist chapel at Eastmoor was
opened in 1821. The congregation moved
to the larger and new premises we see in
the image in 1871. New premises were built
in Norton Road in 1984, and the old chapel
demolished soon after.

For entertainment, the people of Wakefield in 1880 had the choice of a plethora of public houses at which to drink, the temperance bar for those abstaining from alcohol, and for those interested in a cultured night out, this was provided for with the Theatre on Drury Lane, supplemented with the Empire Theatre on Kirkgate after the turn of the century. Many churches and chapels also provided their own evening activities, reading rooms and sports clubs. The coming of the cinema in the years immediately prior to the First World War brought a cheap mass market media and witnessed the building of numerous inner city cinemas such as the Play House on Westgate or conversion of existing buildings into cinemas such as the corn exchange, the Empire Theatre as well as the Theatre Royale and Opera House. A roller rink was also built on Ings road offering a different form of recreational activity. In many ways, a night out in Wakefield in 1900 and 2012 is remarkably similar and bar the convenience foods available in the modern era are a world away from those available in 1900. However in recent decades, all of Wakefield's older cinemas has closed, and many inner city bars and clubs have closed down, along with many of the dance halls like the Embassy Ball Room off Market Street. Wakefield Trinity Rugby Football club moved to its current home in Belle Vue in 1879, where many hundreds of the city's residents then and now support their home team.

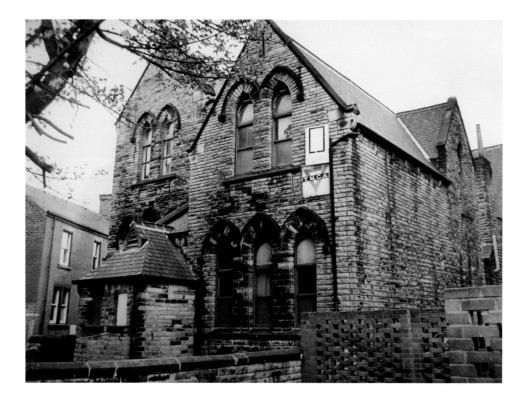

John Street Chapel
Established in the 1870s, the congregation was founded by members of Zion Chapel Chapel on George Street. It closed in 1963.

The Play House Cinema
The Picture House, the first purpose built Cinema in Wakefield.

The Empire Theatre
The Gaumont Cinema on Kirkgate. Built originally as a Theatre by Benjamin Sherwood, the owner of the Theatre Royal, it became a cinema in the years after the First World War.

Today, Wakefield's commercial base as well as its townscape has fundamentally altered: the town is bereft of its mills and pit heads and its manufacturing industry. Industry does remain in the many industrial estates. In the place of mills, factories and open fields are new housing estates to cater for those working elsewhere like Leeds or Bradford or empty office park developments. The city also provides jobs in the bar and leisure industry as well as the IT or service industry. Recent development has seen the new shopping mall of Trinity Walk laid out, a new urban centre at Merchant Gate betwixt Westgate and Balne Lane, as well as the impressive £35 million pound 'The Hepworth Wakefield', named in honour of local sculptress, Barbara Hepworth which opened in May 2011.

Margaret Street
Here we see a leafy Margaret Street in 1881. The street is now far more crowded and has lost its almost rural feel,

1. Communist, Poet and Unitarian

The Revd John Goodwyn Barmby was a Unitarian minister and radical. He has been mostly forgotten in the history of Wakefield and the wider world. Here was a man championing universal suffrage, decades before the more famous Pankhursts. The life and work of Jesus was the over-riding driving force in Goodwyn Barmby's faith, writings and preaching. He was born at Yoxford in Suffolk and was baptised on 12 November 1820. His father, John, a solicitor, married to Julia, died when he was fourteen years old. Goodwyn, he never used his first Christian name had no formal school education but read widely. He eschewed the professions and followed a career of social and political radicalism, reputedly addressing small audiences of agricultural labourers when aged sixteen or seventeen.[1]

Barmby claimed credit for founding the East Suffolk and Yarmouth Chartist council in September 1839. In December, he was elected delegate to the Chartist convention, and in

The Revd John Goodwyn Barmby, Minister at Westgate Chapel from 1858 to 1879.

1   A. L. Morton, *The English utopia*, 1952, pages 132–8. W. H. G. Armytage, *Heavens below: utopian experiments in England, 1560–1960*, 1961, pages 196–207, *The Inquirer*, 29 October 1881, page 721, W. Blazeby, *Unitarian Herald*, 9 November 1881, page 358, G. J. Holyoake, *The history of co-operation*, volume 1, 1875, pages 228–30 and T. Frost, *Forty years' recollections*, 1880.

1840 and 1841, he was re-elected, though alienated from political radicalism by this time.

Already a correspondent of the Owenites' *New Moral World* (writing on language reform and Charles Fourier), in 1840 he visited Paris with a letter of introduction from Owen, and in 1840, he visited Paris, living in the students, quarter and examining for himself the social organisation of the French capital. Here he claimed to have originated the now famous word 'communist' as a translation of the French word *communiste* and popularised the word and its ideals with zeal and fervour. It was Goodwyn Barmby who introduced Engels to the French Communiste movement. Upon his return from Paris, that he described himself as a disciple of Francois Noel BABEUF, Babeuf was probably the first revolutionary communist in history! Babeuf was a prominent revolutionary activist in the great French Revolution of 1789. He advocated and worked for not only political equality but also economic equality. When the Jacobin faction was defeated in 1794 and there was a major shift to the right, Babeuf recognized that the full set of ideals of the Revolution had been betrayed. He took the name Gracchus from two ancient Roman brothers who championed the rights of the poor. He formed a secret revolutionary society, which later became known as the Conspiracy of Equals, and was planning an uprising against the government to take place in May 1796. But the plan was betrayed and Babeuf was arrested and executed. Babeuf was a social utopian, who advocated commonality of ownership, universal suffrage, equality of liberty and justice, equality in finances between all citizens so that all men and women should have the same amount of money. He was also an avowed feminist – as we shall see Babeuf greatly influenced the rest of Goodwyn Barmby's life.

Once back in England, he helped establish a communitorium at Moreville, Hanwell to promote love, intelligence and beauty, to decry the acquisition of vast wealth in the moral name of Jesus Christ but to 'uphold science as the highest authority of man'. He revised orthodox Christianity with a variety of pantheism. Barmby set out to capitalize on the pseudo-Christian undercurrents running through socialism, declaring in his revised Creed, 'I believe ... that the divine is communism, that the demoniac is individualism ...'

Calling himself 'Pontifarch', he announced that he had joined Judaism and 'Christianism' to produce the synthesis of the Communist Church. He devised a four-staged baptismal rite (to symbolize the four stages of history leading to the paradise of universal communism), followed by an anointing with oil. The subtitle of his journal is indicative of his general approach: The Apostle of the Communist Church and the Communitive Life: Communion with God, Communion of the Saints, Communion of Suffrages, Communion of Works and Communion of Goods.

Barmby's explicit infusion of Christian terminology with socialist ideology was adopted by communist propagandists throughout Europe. Communism was touted as the means of bringing to fruition the Christian call for brotherly love. Christ was portrayed trampling the serpent of 'egoism' beneath His feet, surrounded by an army of angels sporting the red caps of the French Revolution.

Members were encouraged to establish agricultural communes and to give up their way of life and income in favour of a communal life. Members were expected to vegetarian and abstain from alcohol. Indeed at one stage, cooked food was not allowed, in favour of a hearty diet of raw vegetables. He remained a lifelong vegetarian and tee-totaller. It was part funded also by his tracts, journals and lecture tours. Indeed, Goodwyn Barmby theorized that humankind developed through four stages of awareness: paradisation, barbarisation, civilisation and finally communitarianism. His self-proclaimed mission was to outline the fourth phase, which itself had four stages going from imperfect community to the perfect community, to the city and then to communist nation.

He married at Marylebone on 4 October 1841 Catherine Isabella Watkins (1816/17–1853), who, under the signature of Kate, contributed to the *New Moral World*. They had a son, Moreville, and a daughter. A passionate support of equality of rights, Both John and Catherine Barmby were early advocate for womens' votes and womens' rights. In the 1840s decades before the Pankhursts, Goodwyn Barmby advocated for right of women to vote. Catherine Barmby in 1843 wrote in a pamphlet demanding the right of women and all men to vote:

> We demand the ecclesiastical emancipation of woman, because from her strong percipient power she has the ability to educate, and thus to benefit society; because the rights of the child demand the ecclesiastical freedom of woman, and because the heart of woman is destined to illumine and hallow the feelings of goodness when addressing itself to the assembly, as the mind or intellect of man is destined to strengthen the being, and to impart to it wisdom. We have the priest, we therefore demand the priestess, the woman teacher of the word, the woman apostle of God's Law!

Here in Wakefield at Westgate, Goodwyn Barmby, true to his nature, supported one of the first women local preachers in the country and perhaps the first female Unitarian lay preacher. A Ms Rolinson was certainly by 1872 an active local preacher, and indeed she had plans to train to be a minister.

In other denominations, women had far few rights. In early British Methodism, a number of women served as local preachers (the heroine of George Elliots Adam Bede is represented as one). However from 1803, women were restricted to addressing women-only meetings – a ban that was not lifted until 1910. It was only from 1918 that Wesleyan Methodism recruited and deployed women Local Preachers on exactly the same basis as men, something us Unitarians appear to have done since 1870. In the Anglican Church, women lay readers were first licensed in 1916. Here, therefore, we have the Unitarians laying the foundations for women lay preachers, ministers and ultimately equal rights to men.

On 13 October 1841, Barmby founded the Communist Propaganda Society and designated 1841 Year 1 of the new communist calendar. The Universal Communitarian Association followed, promoted by the monthly *Educational Circular and Communist Apostle*. In 1842, he founded and almost single handedly wrote the monthly *Promethean*, or *Communitarian Apostle*, which also promoted rational marriage and universal suffrage, and lectured at the 'communist temple' at Marylebone Circus, Marylebone, Middlesex. Out of this activity and through his contact with James Pierrepont Greaves (with whom he published the *New Age*, or *Concordian Gazette*, the journal of Greaves's own Ham Common community), Barmby established the Moreville Communitorium at Hanwell in 1842. The following year, he issued his *Communist Miscellany*, a series of tracts written by

Westgate, *c.* 1910
Looking up Westgate towards the railway station. On the right are the premises of MP Stonehouses.

himself and his wife, and founded the weekly *Communist Chronicle*, which also supported the German communist Wilhelm Weitling.

He soon attracted the backing of radical chartist journalist Thomas Frots. With Frosts backing he wrote 'Book of Platonopolis' combining utopian ideals and scientific projections of a future state of mankind including a peoples' car powdered by steam. He drew up a list of forty-four societarian wants for humanity and a plan of action on an almost global scale. In America, John Wattles founded a Communist Church near Cincinnati based on the principles he had drawn up.

Thomas Frost described Barmby at this time as 'a young man of gentlemanly manners and soft persuasive voice, wearing his light brown hair parted in the middle after the fashion of the Concordist brethren, and a collar and necktie à la Byron'.[2] With the Communitorium renamed the Communist Church by 1844, Barmby began his move towards sectarianism; he conducted a propaganda tour in the north and midlands in the winter of 1845–46 and forged links with the Dublin sect of White Quakers. In 1845, he combined with Frost to revive the Communist Chronicle, for which he translated some of Reybaud's 'Sketches of French socialists', and wrote a philosophical romance entitled *The Book of Platonopolis*, which sought to fuse utopian fiction and modern science. However, Frost soon tired of Barmby's sectarianism, and unbridled utopianism, which in 1844 led him to plan and printing and agriculturual comminitarium across the channel islands of which nothing came, and Frost separated from him in 1846 to establish the *Communist Journal.*

---

2   T. Frost, *Forty years' recollections*, 1880, page 57.

Frost's competition with Barmby destroyed both journals but Barmby continued to proselytize in *Howitt's Journal* and contributed to the *People's Journal*, *Tait's Magazine*, *Chambers's Journal* and other periodicals.

On 22 September 1845, to mark the 53rd anniversary of the French Republic. The congress was in a very real sense the forerunner of the International Working Men's Association, forty-four Communist groups took park in the gathering. Goodwyn Barmby supported the event through his publication the Promethean and Communist Chronicle.

In 1847, he lectured at the Farringdon Hall, Poplar, London, and in July, he convened a meeting at the John Street Institute in support of the Icarian settlements in Texas.

In the new year of 1848, he set up residence on the Isle of Man to publish the 'Apostle'. No one there, or in fact anyone beyond himself and presumably his wife, submitted to the bizaar baptism we mentioned earlier.

As a representative of the Communist Church, he returned to Paris to speak to the Phalansterian club. His journey was portentous as he became involved in the French 1848 revolution which toppled Louis-Philippe the Citizen King and heralded in the Republic once more. Later the same year, after attending a communist conference in London he became disillusioned with communism. It was probably to his friendship with W. J. Fox MP that Barmby owed his introduction to Unitarianism, and thereafter his communitarian interested diminished and was replaced with fervent Unitarianism. He found his intellectual and spiritual origins in Plat, Thomas More, Emanuel Swedenborg and Immanuel Kant, and he was successively minister at Southampton, Topsham, Lympstone, Lancaster and Wakefield.

He was appointed minister of Newbury Presbyterian chapel on 7 November 1849 and was later minister at Frodsom and then at Leonardgate chapel, Lancaster. He entered the Unitarian minister without 'training' and was accorded the title 'Revd'. It is likely he was never ordained.

Westgate Chapel. Oldest Nonconformist Place of Worship in Wakefield Exterior of Westgate Chapel *c.* 1950. Originally entered from a carriage way in Westgate set through a building, the current approach to the building is over shadowed by the Civic Justice Centre, which contrasts starkly and unsympathetically with the graceful lines of John Carr's building.

Interior of Westgate Chapel following the restoration of 1881. The interior remains the same today.

Interior of Westgate Chapel *c.* 1879. The interior as it was from opening in 1752–1880. This is the space that Goodwyn Barmby knew.

The chapel was built in brick between 1750 and 1752, replacing an older one at Westgate End. Originally a place of worship for Protestant Dissenters in the eighteenth century, the chapel is now Unitarian. The roots of the congregation can be traced from the 1630s, and earlier members suffered some ostracism and persecution, but in meeting places, and some of its fittings can be seen in the Westgate Chapel of today. The present chapel was opened in 1752 at a service of dedication to truth which was led by a known unorthodox speaker.

He was one of the best known ministers in the West Riding of Yorkshire and held his post in Wakefield for twenty-one years from June 1858, leading the Wakefield congregation which included the industrialist Henry Briggs. He was also secretary of the West Riding Unitarian Mission. He founded a daughter congregation on Primrose Hill by Kirkgate Station in 1864 and through his 'Band of Faith' movement founded new congregations across the West Riding in Barnsley, Clayton-West, Flockton, Heckmondwike (founded 1864) and other places. A chapel in Ossett was opened in 1867 and closed in 1880. A bazaar was held at the Orangery in 1871 to defray the cost of the iron Church at Ossett. The iron building was given by Mrs Barmby to the congregation and it was later erected in Selby. Through the West Riding Unitarian Mission Society, he was associated in the building of a new chapel in Dewsbury. The cause here was founded 1858 through the efforts of Thomas Todd and rented a chapel on Webster Hill. The new chapel on Swindon Street opened 21 March 1866 and had cost £1700 to build, through the efforts of the Revd P. Cannon. It was closed 1953. The school room at Pepper Hill, Shelf was supported by the society, as were the congregations at Elland and Pudsey where new churches had been built, as well as supporting three missionaries. The Clayton West congregation grew out of the lectures given by Goodwyn Barnby. The Unitarian chapel in Malton was also a beneficiary of his organising skill, as he was involved with a scheme to rejuvenate the congregation and remove the £200 debt on the place.

Westgate, looking towards the Cathedral, c. 1880
Looking up Westgate from Westgate Station, showing the buildings on the southern side of Westgate. Starting from centre left of the image we see the temperance hotel of Herbert Burdett which stood at the junction of Garden Street and Westgate. Thence came The Great Northern Hotel owned by Joe Siswick, Walter Milnthorpe Fishmonger, James Evans Shopkeeper, at 114 Westgate the premises of James Briggs Hosier, John Baker Furniture Dealer as well as the saddler warehouse of Thomas Whitworth. The Elephant & Castle public pouse stood across a small ginell alongside and neighbouring were the premises of George Scott, owner of Scott & Besley Dress Makers. The 122 Westgate was occupied by Mrs Daffarn and Benjamin Walter Kemp, and Milnes Place by Mrs Hunter and Robert Edward Fryer. Dr Thomas Giodarni Wright MD lived in Milnes House, partially visible in this image. Betwixt Milnes House and the Railway Bridge were the premises of John and James Carabine, rug merchants.

On 20 July 1861, Barmby married his second wife, Ada Marianne Shepherd, daughter of the governor of Wakefield gaol, with whom he had a daughter. Ada was related to the Briggs family, and perhaps the adoption of cooperative working by the concern, Henry Briggs Son & Co., was influenced by both familial ties and also by his minister.

Barmby always retained his liberal political convictions and was closely involved in the Wakefield Liberal Association from 1859: he chaired its North Westgate ward committee that year and the full town committee in 1860. Others in the Westgate Chapel congregation could be found in the association, notably Charles Morton. To mark 200 years since the great ejection of 1662, Goodwyn Barmby organised celebrations in Wakefield as

> they [the Unitarians] are the real descendants of the ejected, these 2,000 persons, not having a fixed creed, soon became Arian then Unitarian. They would celebrate it in spite of every opposition.

The following year, he helped found the 'Wakefield Working Men's Institute'.

He spoke with the Mayor and corporation of Wakefield in 1865 at a public meeting held in sympathy on the assassination of President Lincoln. The meeting was held in the Court House on Wood Street, chaired by Alderman Lee, the then mayor. Goodwyn Barmby noted that Lincoln was a great and good man, martyred for his loyalty to duty. He was the only minister of religion to speak at the meeting. The same year he, along with Henry Briggs and Daniel Gaskell, was elected to the committee for the Liberal Candidates standing in the South West Riding during the General Election of that year. Furthermore, 1865 witnessed a public meeting being held in Wakefield for Religious Freedom, championing the disestablishment of the Church of England. At the meeting, Goodwyn Barmby proposed that members of the Church of England injuriously affected the liberty of other religious bodies, in which he was supported by the Revd J. S. Eastmead of Salem Chapel. Both he and Eastmead sat on the Local Board of Education Examination Board of the Mechanics Institution, from 1859, for Wakefield along with Eastmead as chairman in 1860 and G. W. Harrison. Dr S. Holdsworth was chair in 1861, Eastmead remained on

W. S. Banks
W. S. Banks colleague of Goodwyn Barmby on the committee of the Wakefield Mechanics Institute and for a time a Unitarian. He is best remember for his book *Walks about Wakefield*.

the board until 1863, when he was joined T. W. Gissing, Chemist and W. S. Banks. He was committee member of Wakefield Mechanics Institution from 1859.

In 1867, he organised a large public meeting in Wakefield in support of parliamentary reform and joined the National Association for Women's Suffrage. The Wakefield Committee of the National Society for Woman's Suffrage was founded with Ms Julia Barmby as secretary, in 1872. Sadly with Barmby leaving Wakefield, the Wakefield branch of the society was wound up in 1882. Barmby was a member of the council of Mazzini's International League and also supported Polish, Italian and Hungarian freedom. In 1870, he was a founder of the Wakefield branch of the RSPCA; 1873 witnessed Goodwyn Barmby establish a Wakefield branch of the National Republican Brotherhood, supported by Mr Skipworth, solicitor of Wakefield. The object of the brotherhood was universal adult suffrage, proportional representation in the House of Common, Disestablishment of the Church of England, free compulsory secular education and nationalisation of land as well as the founding of a social democratic and federal republic. In July 1877, he was appointed a member of the General Committee of Clayton Hospital, along with W. S. Banks, who for a time was a fellow Unitarian. This body oversaw the building of the current premises on Northgate. He had been involved in the building of the Albert Wing and its opening in 1863.

The Albert Wing of Clayton Hospital, Wood Street, c. 1880
The Albert Wing of Clayton Hospital, erected as the towns memorial to Prince Albert. Medical treatment was provided for the people of Wakefield by two medical charities, the House of Recovery (1826–53) and the Clayton Hospital and Wakefield General Dispensary founded in 1787, along with an increasing number of private doctors and medical men. Clayton Hospital is named after Thomas Clayton, a mayor of Wakefield and was founded in 1854. It was an amalgamation of Wakefield General Dispensary, founded in 1787, and the Wakefield House of Recovery, founded in 1826. Wakefield General Dispensary was for outpatients, and the Wakefield House of Recovery was for poor inpatients suffering from infectious diseases. In 1852, the Wakefield Union Workhouse was completed and its hospital wards accommodated pauper invalids and fever cases, so that the House of Recovery was closed in 1854. In 1863, Mayor Clayton financed an expansion and the institution was renamed 'The Clayton Hospital and Wakefield General Dispensary'. The site moved from Dispensary Yard to the present site in 1876, and the new building was opened in 1879

Clayton Hospital, Northgate, c. 1920
The 1879 buildings of Clayton
Hospital. Goodwyn Barmby was
a committee member of the body
which ran the establishment.

Barmby wrote several volumes of pastoral poetry: *The Poetry of Home and Childhood* (1853), *Scenes of Spring* (1860) and *The Return of the Swallow* (1864). His devotional works included *Aids to Devotion* (1865), the *Wakefield Band of Faith Messenger* (1871–79), which was committed to the advance of theological liberalism, and a large number of hymns and tracts.

He was struck down in the pulpit on chirstmas day 1878 and was unable to take any further services. It seems he had a stroke. He retired to Yoxford but continued to hold intensely devotional private services. He died there on 18 October 1881 and was buried at the cemetery of Framlingham, Suffolk. His second wife survived. His obituary in the Leeds Mercury describes him as

an ardent liberal, his last act previous to leaving Wakefield was to vote for Mr Mackie at the last General Election. Mr Barmby was at all times the warm friend of the working classes, while his sympathy and charity were unbounded; and many will gratefully remember his kindness and acknowledge his worth.

The 1737 Pulpit of Westgate Chapel
The pulpit of Westgate Chapel. It was first used
in 1737 in the congregations' chapel on Westgate
Common. It was moved to the current building
in 1752, when the current Westgate Chapel was
opened. It was here that Revd John Goodwyn Barmby
preached his laster sermon on Christmas Day 1878.

2. What's in a Name?

Gaskell Street is named after members of the Gaskell Family, who were prominent citizens of Wakefield. Benjamin and Daniel Gaskell in their own life times affected changes and improvements to education and other causes in Wakefield and Yorkshire as a whole. Both brothers were members of Parliament, indeed Daniel was the first MP for Wakefield. Yet both men have slipped out of the consciousness of Wakefield's past, and few people have heard of either men. Benjamin Gaskell was MP for Maldon in Essex and championed education in Wakefield, founding two schools and a Sunday school. The schools lived on after his death. Many people perhaps have not heard of Benjamin Gaskell.

Benjamin Gaskell was a man who lived out his Unitarian religious conviction. A man who deserves to be remembered. He lies beneath our feet in the catacombs, and his

Mr Benjamin Gaskell
Portrait of Benjamin
Gaskell, executed in the
1830s. MP from 1807 to
1826, he lived at Thornes
House, Wakefield.

funerary monument can be found on the walls of Westgate Chapel. In death, he has been over shadowed by his younger brother, Daniel Gaskell.

Benjamin Gaskell was born on 28 February 1781, first son of Daniel Gaskell of Clifton Hall, near Manchester by Hannah, daughter of James Noble of Lancaster.
Educated *at* Gateacre, near Liverpool; between 1796 and 1797, he attended Manchester Academy a Unitarian educational establishment founded in 1789 as part of Moseley Street Chapel, which moved to Upper Brook Street in 1839. The congregation had been opened by Rev William Turner, minister of Westgate Chapel. Benjamin then studied under the radical Revd Thomas Belsham at New College Hackney. Class mates of Benjamin Gaskell were the radical William Hazlitt as well as Charles Wellbeloved who became minister at York Unitarian Chapel.

Under Belsham, from 1798 to 1800, the young Benjamin Gaskell was taught Greek, Latin and Hebrew, as well as mathematics, science, history and government. He then studied BA at Trinity College. Cambridge starting in 1800.He Joined Lincolns Inn in 1804.

With the death of his great uncle, James Milnes, he inherited the formers estates. The will decreed that Benjamin would inherit Thornes House, as long as provision was made for Daniel to have his own estate, resulting in the purchase of Lupset Hall. Daniel had lived at

Mr Daniel Gaskell
Daniel Gaskell younger brother of Benjamin Gaskell. First MP for Wakefield in 1833–37. He lived at Lupset Hall.

Thornes House with James Milnes as a companion since the death of James Milne's wife. The Milnes family had been associated with Westgate Chapel and its congregation since the start of the eighteenth century and had been instrumental in building the new chapel of 1750.

Benjamin married, on 17 June 1807, Mary Brandreth of Broad Green Hall, Liverpool. Their son James Milnes Gaskell was baptised at Thornes House by the Minister of Westgate Chapel Revd Johnstone. A second son was born on 4 September 1809, but the child died soon after birth. In 1806, he stood for Maldon in Essex, associating himself

Thornes House, built by James Milnes Jnr

Thornes House, home of James Milnes and later Benjamin Gaskell, was a fine Georgian mansion built in 1779–82 for the James Milnes family by Horbury architect James Carr.

It was arguably the most imposing eighteenth century building in the city. It was one of twenty-seven buildings in the British Isles to be included in the 1802 edition of 'Vitruvius Brittanica' a regular survey of the world's most important buildings by one George Richardson published 1802–08.

In 1919, the estate was put up for sale and bought by the Corporation for £18,500. The plans were to use 20 acres and the house for a school and use the remaining 92 acres to build an estate of 750 council houses. The Corporation badly needed the houses and it also needed the work for the considerable numbers of local unemployed.

The Housing Commission, however, would not approve the project so it eventually opened as a park on 2 August 1924. The houses were built at Lupset later. Work was found for some of the unemployed who were used to make the paddling pool, tennis courts and pathway at the Horbury Road end of the park.

Meanwhile, the school was founded in 1921 as separate boys and girls secondary schools which made use of Wakefield Technical College for the first year. The schools then moved to the Thornes House site in 1922.

In 1941, the two schools were united under one headmaster, and in 1944, the school became a Grammar School under the new Education Act.

Most of the original house was destroyed by a fire in 1951 thanks possibly to the Wakefield Amateur Theatre Guild which was storing costumes for their Thornes Park production of Midsummer Night's Dream in a room in the school which was the seat of the fire according to the official report. A dropped cigarette end among the costumes was given as a likely cause. New buildings were soon constructed, fitted out by the Wakefield firm of Drake & Warters, and came into use in 1956.

Memorial to James Milnes, Westgate Chapel

Memorial window to James Milnes MP in Westgate Chapel, Wakefield. Milnes, heir to a wealthy Wakefield woollen merchant, was not interested in trade. On the death of his father, a religious dissenter and a prominent local supporter of Pitt, he soon showed contrary political tendencies too: Michael Angelo Taylor informed William Adam, 9th October 1794, 'By the way, Mr James Milnes who bought Egremont House will purchase and vote with us, and he desired to speak about it'. At the general election of 1796, evidently at the instigation of Lord Lauderdale, Milnes was lured into a contest for Shaftesbury, in company with William Dawson, whose family had been business associates of his. Told that the outlay would probably be £4,000, he paid most of the estimated cost of failure (£17,000). He was High Sherrif of Yorkshire 1800–01. In 1802, he purchased a quiet seat on the Kenrick interest.

Milnes was an inconspicuous member. He joined Brooks's Club, sponsored by Fox, on 17 May 1803 and a week later voted with the Whigs on the failure of negotiations to prevent the resumption of war with France. He appeared in some lists of the minority for Pitt's naval motion, 15th March 1804. Pitt's calculators listed him 'Prince' in September. He died 21 April 1805. He is buried in the catacombs beneath Westgate Chapel.

The great William Wilberforce described him on a visit to Thorne's House in 1795 as 'good natured and well intentioned' and an obituary commended his 'urbanity of manners and inflexible integrity in public and private life'.

with the promotion of a new charter for the borough: he narrowly won the seat but was unseated on petition and defeated by Western at the ensuing general election. He became MP for Maldon in 1812.

In 1815 with the return of Napoleon to rule France, 1st May 1815, Benjamin Gaskell was one of several MPs who supported a petition for peace, stating:

> the petitioners cannot but consider any attempt to dictate to France, or any other country, the form or mode of its government, the person who shall or shall not be at the head of such government, or in any way to interfere in its internal policy and regulations, as highly impolitic and manifestly unjust: The petitioners, therefore, deprecate any designs to involve this country in a war for such an object, a war against those principles which this nation has always maintained and acted upon;

Tomb of James Milnes in Westgate Chapel Catacombs
James Milnes lies entombed in the catacombs of Westgate Chapel. They are one of the earliest sets of public catacombs in the country, and date, in part, from the building of the chapel in 1750. They were extended in 1808.

Portrait of Revd Johnstone
Thomas Johnston (1786–1856) was educated under Belsham at Hackney from 1788 to 1789. He was appointed as minister at Westgate in 1792. He married the daughter of John Miilnes of Flockton Hall in 1793. He married for a second time in 1831, Elizabeth Lumb, his first wife having died in 1828. He is buried in the catacombs beneath Westgate Chapel.

In this motion to retain peace in Europe, he stood shoulder to shoulder with Samuel Whitbread, Sir Francis Burdett, George Tierney and many other prominent Whig members of parliament. The Whigs could not prevent the war, and the battle of Waterloo sealed the fate of France and Napoleon.

Following Waterloo, he voted with the Whigs, who had the majority, against the property tax, 18 March 1816, he proceeded to vote for reductions in public and royal expenditure, voted against the unconstitutional use of the military which had been used to curb civil unrest, 13 May 1816. On 20 May 1817, he voted for Burdett's motion for parliamentary reform. He was in the minority on the choice of a new Speaker, 2 June 1817. On 13th and 15 April 1818, he opposed the ducal marriage grants. He voted for the repeal of the Septennial Act, 19 May 1818, and for Brougham's motion for an inquiry into popular education, 3 June.

Early in 1818, when the Whigs thought of intervening at Maldon, Peter Du Cane informed Lord Holland that Gaskell (whom he described as 'the Whig Member') had 'uniformly voted so well since his return that I should have felt great diffidence in risking his return for the sake of my own'. He was duly re-elected in 1818. In January 1819, he took residence in Upper Brook Street London for the remainder of the 'season' of balls and round of socialising that took place in the new year. He remained in London till August 1821, when he left for Thornes House.

He voted for an inquiry into Peterloo massacre, 16 May 1821, and the remission of Henry Hunt's prison sentence, 22 March and 24 April 1822. He was in the minorities condemning the prosecution of the Methodist missionary John Smith in Demerara, 11 June 1824, and the Jamaican slave trials, 2 March 1826. He voted for the licensing of public houses, 27 June 1822, and tithe reform, 6 June 1825. He retired at the dissolution in June 1826, having given notice of this intention nine months earlier, when he stated that *circumstances over which I have no control ... would probably interfere very much with the discharge of my duty*.

Memorial of Revd Johnstone
Upon his death, Thomas Johnstone was buried beneath Westgate Chapel. A fitting resting place for the man who had been minister for over 40 years.

Gaskell lived abroad, 1827–28, but thereafter led 'a life of quiet retirement and unostentatious goodness' at Thornes, where William Ewart Gladstone, the Eton and Christ Church friend of his only child James Milnes Gaskell (1810–73), Conservative Member for Wenlock, 1832–68, was a guest in 1829 and 1832. When Gladstone returned there in 1871, he experienced 'a vivid recollection of the place as it was associated with much kindness received and with my first stepping out from a very retired childhood and youth into the world'. Indeed, Mr and Mrs Gaskell and Daniel Gaskell appear several times in Gladstone's numerous diaries.

Gladstone was drawn to Gaskell's wife, who mothered and inspired him, by a common interest in religion Gaskell, whose brother Daniel was Liberal Member for Wakefield, 1832–37. Both Benjamin and Daniel were subscribers to Lady Hewley's charity, to which remit was the training of Unitarian Ministers at Manchester College York, along with the Revd Charles Beloved of York, the Revd William Turner, Revd Thomas Johnstone as well as John Pemberton Heywood, another Wakefield man. Indeed Benjamin Gaskell was president of the charity from August 1815 to August 1817. He is recorded as donating £10 a year to the charity.

In education locally, he supported an Infant school of box sexes for sixty children which he had established in 1829. In addition, he supported a girls' school capable of teaching thirty-five, as well as supporting a Sunday school, which taught sixty children. Both he and his brother were governors of York Pauper Lunatic Assylum. In 1824, 1825 and 1826, he subscribed to the Yorkshire Musical Festival, which raised funds for the York County Hospital as well as the General Infirmaries of Leeds, Hull and Sheffield. He is perhaps best known as supporting the foundation of St Jame's church Thornes in 1830. On 26 July 1830, he was commissioned as Deputy Lord Lieutenant of Yorkshire, along with Samuel Stocks, a prominent Wakefield Wesleyan Methodist.[3] In September 1835,

---

3   The *Standard Wednesday*, 27 July 1831, p. 1.

Parish Church of St James, Thornes, *c.* 1880
Thornes Church, founded by Mr and
Mrs Benjamin Gaskell. Many are unaware that
this Anglican place of worship was co-founded
by a Unitarian, albeit one who attended services
at Wakefield parish church as it then was in the
Presbyterian manner.

York Minster held a festival of music to celebrate the anniversary of the coronation of the king, beginning on 8 September 1835 for three days. Benjamin Gaskell was one of the many subscribers to fund the event.[4] In 1839, Lord Morpeth and the Bishop of Ripon were guests at Thornes House.[5] Mary Gaskell, wife of Benjamin Gaskell, died suddenly on the 23 November 1845 at Weetwood Hall, near Leeds aged sixty-three. Of interest between 1835 and 1845, Benjamin Gaskell had not signed the trustees minutes of Westgate Chapel, so clearly was not at the meetings, but following his wife's death, he starts to sign the minutes again and presumably to attend meetings and services. In 1846, he is recorded as supporting Wakefield Mechanics institute and donating land for a cricket pitch.[6]

In January 1847, both he and his brother Daniel gave £50 each towards alleviating the effects of the famine in Ireland. In total, Wakefield raised £350 for famine relief in Ireland, then a very large sum of money. One of the last acts in his life was the giving of £105 towards the building of Lancaster Mechanics institute.[7] His brother Daniel gave £35, and the Revd Goodwyn Barmby a modest £1. Goodwyn Barmby was then a Unitarian Minister in Lancaster and would in 1858 move to Wakefield, a move perhaps brought through the Lancaster Mechanics Institute. Barmby would become a committee member of the Wakefield Mechanics Institute. He attended the trustees meeting of

Westgate Chapel of 19 January 1857. He died two days later. His obituary reads:

Wentworth House
On the left, we see Wentworth House and then open fields leading to St John's. The house was built in 1802–03 by John Pemberton Heywood, a barrister, and lived in by him until his death in 1835 and subsequently by his wife until 1851. The house, its grounds and outbuildings were bought in 1878 for the considerable sum of £8000 to establish a girls' high school which opened in the same year. J. P. Heywood is buried in the catacombs beneath Westgate Chapel.

---

4   The *York Herald and General Advistor*, 29 August 1835.
5   The *Morning Post*, 11 September 1839.
6   The *Leeds Mercury*, 29 August 1846.
7   *Lancaster Gazette*, 29 December 1855.

BENJAMIN GASKELL, Esq. Jan. 21. At Thornes House, near Wakefield, in his 75th year, Benjamin Gaskell, esq. formerly M. P. for Maldon. He was born on the 28th Feb. 1781, the elder son of Daniel Gaskell, esq. of Clifton Hall, near Manchester, by Hannah, daughter of James Noble, esq. of Lancaster, and was educated at Gateacre, near Liverpool, and at Trinity College, Cambridge. He was first returned to Parliament for Maldon, at the general election of 1806, and some circumstances connected with this return are worth recalling. The poll (Oct. 30, 1806) was as follows:–For Col. Strutt (the father of the present Lord Rayleigh), 63; Mr. Gaskell, 31; Charles Callis Western, esq. (the late Lord Western), 29. A petition was presented by Mr. Western, complaining of an undue election, and the committee, appointed Feb. 4, 1807, decided against Mr. Gaskell's return, and gave the seat to Mr. Western. The votes of the committee were equal, and the decision was arrived at by the casting vote of the chairman, Sir Gilbert Heathcote, who not only gave a casting, but a double vote. Mr. Simeon, M.P. for Reading, who was Mr. Gaskell's nominee on the committee, brought before the House of Commons the manner in which he had been unseated, but no further steps were taken in the matter. At the general election which took place in May, 1807, on the dissolution of Lord Grenville's government, Mr. Gaskell again stood for Maldon, and was defeated by two votes, the numbers being—for Strutt, 58; Western, 29; and Gaskell, 27. During the interval before the next election Mr. Gaskell was mainly instrumental in procuring for Maldon the restoration of its charter. He was returned without opposition in 1812, and remained unopposed till he quitted the House of Commons in 1826. Mr. Gaskell was a moderate whig in politics. He was strongly opposed to the imposition of civil disabilities on account of religious opinions, and was a zealous friend to Catholic emancipation, supporting the various motions of Mr. Canning, Mr. Grattan, and Mr. Plunkett on that subject. He voted with Mr. Brougham on the question of education; with Lord John Russell and Mr. Abercromby for a temperate reform in the representation; and was a consistent supporter of Sir Samuel Romilly and Sir James Mackintosh in their endeavours to mitigate the severity of our criminal code. He was generally disposed, however, to support the government of the day in all matters affecting the honour and security of the country, and was always ready to place a generous construction upon the motives and conduct of public men, never concurring in any proposition which had the appearance of vindictiveness, and rarely supporting any motion that went to harass or inculpate others. In 1826 Mr. Gaskell retired from parliament, and resided abroad from the summer of 1827 till the autumn of 1828. He afterwards resided chiefly at Thornes House, leading a life of quiet retirement and unostentatious goodness, to which there is no lack of those who can bear grateful testimony. Subsequently to the death of Mrs. Gaskell, in November, 1845, this disposition for retirement increased upon him; and his chief social intercourse was latterly that of his own hospitable dinner table and drawing-room, where the ease of friendly intercourse was ever happily blended with the most graceful observances of wealth and station. On the 17th June, 1807, he married Mary, the eldest daughter of the late Dr. Brandreth, of Liverpool. Their only surviving issue is James Milnes Gaskell, esq. M.P., who married, in May, 1832, Mary, the second daughter of the late Right Hon. C. W. Williams Wynn, M.P. by whom he has issue.

Tomb of Benjamin Gaskell, Westgate Chapel
The tomb of Benjamin Gaskell in the catacombs of Westgate Chapel. He lies alongside his brother, who was returned in 1875 with special permission from the Home Office.

Memoiral to Benjamin Gaskell
Memorial to Benjamin Gaskell, erected in Westgate Chapel by his son. Something of his character is presented in the wording on the monument.

3. Street of Six Churches

George Street, in the City Centre of Wakefield, is not an ancient street of the Medieval town, it was created in the 1780s. Up until the 1960s, the street, if we included Fair Ground Road remarkably boasted no less than six places of worship within 500 feet of each other as well as no less than eight public houses. The oldest of these places of worship was built before George Street existed.

Thornhill Street

Not strictly speaking being on George Street but situated a little distance back from the road was Thornhill Street Methodist Chapel.

The foundation stones were laid by John Wesley on 30 August 1773. The '*new house* [chapel]' (cost the sum of £500 to build, £202 of which having already been raised. In 1775, £250 was borrowed from Mr James Milnes and £50 from Francis Scott to pay for the chapel.

Internally the chapel was lit by candles, with a large chandelier in the centre of the roof, with tin sconces on the walls between the windows, with a gallery to the rear of the building where the orchestra played from.

The chapel was opened on Thursday 8 April 1774 by John Wesley, exactly twenty-two years after he had preached in the parish church. His diary entry for the day reads:

> Opened the New House at Wakefield. What a change is here, since our friend was afraid to let me preach in his house lest the mob should pull it down!. So I preached in the main street, and there was sown the first seed which has since born so plenteous Harvest

Wesley next preached in the chapel two months later on 4 July, 12 June 1777 and 28 April 1779. His next visit came a year later on 10 April when he preached to a 'genteel' congregation. Thursday 9th May 1782 saw Wesley again preach in Wakefield.

I preached in Wakefield in the evening. Such attention sat on every face that it seemed as if everyone in the congregation was on the brink of Believing

Wesley's last visit to Wakefield was on 23 April 1790, just under a year before his death at his home in London.

In 1795 saw a second preacher's house being built, the trustees having to resort to borrowing to pay for the building works. In May 1799, it was decided that a suitable system of seat rents should be introduced. As the front seats were the most valuable they were let at 5s 6d per quarter, the corner pews being the cheapest at 2s 6d per quarter. In 11 January 1800 saw Dr Alexander Disney give a sermon, and in the same year, William Walton a trustee of the chapel was appointed Chief Constable of Wakefield. The famous Dr Coke preached at the close of 1801 for the benefit of the friends and strangers society.

The service commenced at 6:00 a.m., and it was also advertised that Mr Wydle and the Choir would be in attendance as well.

By 1800, it was becoming increasingly apparent that a new chapel would have to be built as the existing structure and site had no scope for enlargement or development. The circuit purchased the site of a new chapel in the fashionable development of South Parade from Mr George Charnock for the sum of £537 1s 2d. The building of the circuit's first chapel commenced soon after. In a few short years, chapels would be built across the circuit. The building became occupied by the Quakers. The first meeting of the Wakefield Quakers was held on Sunday 27 January 1716. Eventually, the Society purchased this house and held their meetings there until May 1772, when it, with the adjoining garden, was sold for £320, more suitable premises having being found at Agbrigg, situated on the north side of Wakefield – Doncaster Road; the yard adjoining upon the Lane Syde being registered by Quaker Sessions in January 1694–95 as a place of burial for the people called Quakers. This property is opposite the present cemetery, and the old house still bears a stone with the date 1772 carved thereon, but it is now converted into cottages. The four archways, now filled up, are said to have been for the stabling of those who came by conveyances from a distance. In the year 1785, owing to the smallness of the Agbrigg meeting it and the one at Ackworth were combined, which arrangement continued until 1793, when a separate meeting was established for Wakefield. When the Weslyans removed to their new chapel in 1805, the one they had used in Thornhill Street since John Wesley laid the foundation stone on 30 August 1772 was sold to the friends for £500, who proceeded to take out the pews and galleries and adapt the building for their requirements. Twenty years later, they were able to purchase a plot of the adjoining land, comprising 500 years, at 10s 6d for the use as a burial ground.

Many well-known Wakefield families have been connected with the Society of Friends, Lumb, Aldam, Leatham, Benington, Holdsworth, Kitching, Spence, Binks and Wallis. John Bright married Margaret Leatham, sister of Edward Aldam Leatham and William Henry Leathem, at the Friends' Meeting House in Thornhill Street on 10 July 1847.

West Parade Wesleyan Chapel

Set back from George Street at the end of West Parade, stood between 1802 and 1972 West Parade Chapel. It was designed as part of a fashionable new housing develop of South Parade. The building cost the sum of £3,842 to build and was opened in March 1802. It is interesting to note that many of the tradesmen who built the chapel also subscribed towards the building fund.

A large part of the chapel income at this time came from pew rents. In September 1804, 286 seats in the body of the chapel were let at £36 16s 6d per quarter and 461 college seats for £61 3s 4 ½d, making a quarterly income of £97 19s 10 ½d.

The old chapel was sold at auction to the Quakers, with their £500 being received in January 1805, which allowed the trust to pay the £80 owing to Mrs Bamlford in the March of the same year. July 1805 saw a subscription book opened to build a manse; £50 each were given by William Walton, John Tootal, Joseph Holdsworth and William Spicer. Altogether twenty-one people subscribed, raising £435 12s, towards the £716

18s 6d needed. More money was borrowed again in 1807, £100 from William Spicer, £50 from Joseph Scott, £50 and then a further £43 was given by Joseph Holdsworth. All of these people were repaid when the chapel was reseated and a new system of rents was introduced.

The pew rents were raised in January 1808, as the chapel was heavily in debt to its creditors. As the gallery had the most fashionable seats, the front seats were let at 1s 6d per quarter, the second and third rows at 2s per quarter and the fourth and fifth at 1s 6d with the remained at 1s per quarter. In the body of the chapel, the eight back rows were let at 1s 6d per quarter, the rest of the side pews 2s 6d per quarter and those in the central block of pews at 2s or 1s 6d per quarter depending on its position. It was decided in January 1821 that £12 be allotted from the chapel fund to the town stewards to defray the cost of lighting the chapel with gas. In the December, it was agreed to loan Kirkhamgate School the sum of £20 as they were in arrears and gave the school an annual gift of £5. In the following year, it was agreed that an organ was to be set up in the chapel, the cost to be defrayed through subscriptions. This was only possible as the conference only allowed the large chapels to erect organs in 1820, only to guide congregational singing, only where orchestra were in existence. An approved organist was appointed with the salary of 10 guineas a year, and the blower at £1 a year. The organ was opened in January 1824 by Edward Booth, the organist of Holy Trinity Church Leeds. The instrument had been built by Joseph Booth of Wakefield and was placed in the semicircular recess at the southern end of the chapel, which was originally used by the choir.

In the early 1830s, the trustees decided to enlarge and renovate the chapel. Works commenced in 1835 and were completed by 1838. The works saw the chapel being lengthened from 66 feet to 96 feet, the total cost of the work being £937, of which £912 6s had been raised through subscription and donations, £100 was received from Samuel Stocks and £50 each from Joseph Holdsworth and Joshua Swallow. Unlike when the chapel was built, few of the workmen subscribed and this time the amounts were small. The chapel was opened for divine worship on Friday 19 October 1838. To mark the centenary of Methodism, a new pipe organ was installed and opened on Wednesday 6 March, by its builder, Mr Francis Booth of Wakefield. Other activities took place later in the year when a four day event was held in the corn exchange, commencing on Friday 25 November. Early in 1880, the renovation of the chapel was begun. The pews were made alike and the choir vestries and vestibule were added. A new gallery facade was installed and was made out of selected pitch pine with Mahogany detail, a new Mahogany and gilt brass common rail was installed and the organ was enlarged to three manuals by I Abbott of London. During the alterations, a Harmonium was used instead of the organ. The renovation scheme cost the some of £3,060 and was completed in 1882. This had been entirely met by subscriptions, bazaars, etc. Enough money was raised through supplementary efforts to remove the £300 debt on the school and the £1,100 debt on the chapel. The chapel was opened for divine service on 1 January 1881 by the Revd Brook.

The chapel celebrated its 150th anniversary from 2 April to 9 April 1952, with the anniversary sermon being preached by the Revd Prof Cecil Pawson MBE MSC FRCS, who was the Vice President of the Conference. However by the late 1950s, West Parade was something of a white elephant. The congregation was declining; it was a declining church in a declining part of the city where the population was moving out to the housing estates on the edge of the city. Some blocks of flats were built in the area, but they did little to provide new members, the congregation standing at 102 persons by 1963. The building was badly in need of renovation and would cost about £4,000. Various schemes were put forward to save the chapel, including creating a City Centre Chapel, by merging West Parade, Grove Road, Eastmoor and Brunswick. The plan came to nothing and West Parade was closed on Sunday 9 October 1966 by the Revd W. H. Dixon.

The building was purchased by the Corporation who demolished the chapel and school in 1974.

West Parade Chapel
West parade Chapel viewed from South Parade in 1880. The vast size of the building is evident in this image.

Façade of West Parade Chapel, *c.* 1880
The simple and handsome façade of West Parade Chapel. The building was designed by the Doncaster Architect Charles Watson, who also designed St John's Parish Church, Wakefield and the Country Court on Wood Street.

West Parade Chapel was closed in 1966 and demolished in 1972 and replaced by the mundane 'White Rose House', which spoils the setting of South Parade and robbed Wakefield of one of its finest buildings.

Interior of West Parade, *c.* 1879
Interior of West Parade Chapel
as it was between 1838 and
the restoration of 1880. The
building could seat almost
2,000 persons, making it by far
the largest place of worship in
Wakefield.

Interior of West Parade Chapel,
1902
The interior of West Parade
following the restoration of 1880.
The restoration also witnessed
the rebuilding of the chapels pipe
organ which dated back to 1824.
The pewing and gallery façade
were in polish mahogany.

South Parade as it was, *c.* 1880

Running from west to east and backing on to George Street is South Parade, a fine Georgian terrace, erected from 1786 to 1827 on land owned by the Charnock and Johnson family's. Unlike St John's North, the frontages were not of uniform design as the development was piecemeal. In 1803 plan to extend the scheme at right angles to South Parade and infill the gaps between the then standing houses on South Parade with buildings of a uniform design drawn up by Charles Watson. Then fulcrum of the two streets was to be West Parade Wesleyan chapel. The scheme was never completed in full, but did see the construction of the chapel and Nos 7 to 9 South Parade. By 1795, a road was opened up into the White Bear Yard in Westgate to serve the development, later named Queen Street.

Burneytops House and the Wesleyan Manse, West Parade, *c.* 1905

The Manse on West Parade stands alongside Burneytops House, built for a member of the Charnock family in the 1770s. The oldest part of the Manse date back to 1805. It was enlarged in 1870. The MacDonald sisters were four Scottish sisters, notable for their marriages to well-known people of the Victorian era. Alice, Georgiana, Agnes and Louisa were perhaps the most famous residents of the Manse. There were eleven children in the Macdonald family: seven daughters and four sons. Mary (1834–36) was the firstborn; followed by Henry (1836–91), called Harry, who introduced his younger sisters Georgiana and Agnes to his artistic friends, known as the Birmingham Set; then Alice; Caroline (1838–54); Georgiana; Frederic William (1842–1928); Agnes; Louisa; Walter (1847–47); Edith (1848–1937), who never married and lived at home until her mother's death; and Herbert (1850–51). Their parents were the Reverend George Browne MacDonald (1805–68), a Wesleyan Methodist minister who was at West Parade (1844–46) and Hannah Jones (1809–75).

Alice (1837–1910) was born on 4th April in Sheffield. She married John Lockwood Kipling and was the mother of Rudyard Kipling. Lord Dufferin once said, 'Dullness and Mrs. Kipling cannot exist in the same room'.

Georgiana's (1840–1920) father was moved by the Methodist Conference to a Birmingham Circuit and it was here that Georgie was born on 28th July 1840. She married the pre-Raphaelite painter Edward Burne-Jones. She became the mother-in-law of John William Mackail and grandmother of Angela Thirkell and Denis Mackail. Agnes (1843–1906) married the president of the Royal Academy Edward Poynter. Louisa (1845–1925) married the industrialist Alfred Baldwin and was the mother of prime minister Stanley Baldwin and grandmother to Oliver and Arthur Baldwin. Louisa wrote novels, short stories and poetry, sometimes credited as 'Mrs. Alfred Baldwin'.

Zion Congretional Church

It was not until the last quarter of the eighteenth century that the Independents made any endeavour to form a Congregational church in Wakefield, though for some years the Revds Sugden, Gallon and Sutcliffe used to visit the town and preach at the house of

John Thompson, next door to the Playhouse in Westgate, who with his nephew Samuel Thompson were the founders of Independency in Wakefield.

In 1778, the Revd Mr Ralph preached in this house; being threatened for preaching in an unlicensed house on the following Sunday he preached in the house of Thomas Wood at Flanshaw to a large assembly. In 1781, the Revd James Wrath, of Bolton, then visiting Wakefield, preached during the week at his brother's house. He offered to preach again on the Sunday following, but his brother, being afraid of a disturbance, declined. Thomas Ward, however, of Flanshaw Hall, opened his doors to Wrath, and a few inhabitants of Alverthorpe became interested in the gospel. Afterwards a room was taken in Wakefield, at the bottom of the Great Bull yard, the Revd James Scott, of Heckmondwike, the Revd S. Tapp, S. Cave (connected by family with Wakefield) and other ministers, conducting service there. The number of the people increased, though very gradually, and the congregation resolved to build a chapel.

In 1782, it was decided to take the corn barn at the bottom of the Great Bull Yard as a meeting house, where the Revd William Tapp officiated. On 1 January 1783, the new chapel at the bottom of Rodney Yard was opened by the Revd John Cockin and Thomas Grove.

A church was formed in April 1783, when the pastor and members signed 'a solemn covenant,' which still remains extant in the church records. The first sacrament was administered on the first Sunday in June 1783 to eighteen members (including Mr and Mrs Bruce). Nearly 176 members were admitted during the pastorate of Mr Bruce.

The Revd Samuel Bruce was born near Heckmondwike in 1754 and educated at the Academy there under the Revd James Scott. His first call was to Grimsby, but when riding through the town on this way to Pontefract, where he had received a call, preached in the room in the Great Bull Yard and immediately was invited to the pastorate at Wakefield, which he accepted, 13 October 1782, in preference to Pontefract. Under his forceful ministration, the congregation greatly increased, the barn was soon found to be inadequate and a plot of land was purchased on 22 October 1782, of the sum of £70, and the erection of Zion chapel was at once proceeded with. The new building was opened on 1st January 1783, being generally then known as 'Bruce's chapel'. He remained at Wakefield for forty-four years but was disabled by a paralytic stroke in 1826 and died on 1st June 1833, aged seventy-eight. In 1844, the current church building was erected. It is now flats.

Zion Chapel, George Street, *c.* 1880
The foundation stone of Zion chapel was laid on 20 July 1843. William Shaw was responsible for the design and was one of the major benefactors. Today Zion chapel is a block of apartments.

Salem Independent Chapel
In 1799, with the growth of the congregation at Zion becoming too small, the building was enlarged. However as a result of these improvements, differences in opinion arose as to the rearrangement and allotment of pews, secession took place, and a new chapel (Salem) was built in George Street. The first meetings of the breakaway group were held in a room in Old Crown Yard Northgate, under the ministration of the Revd Benjamin Rayson. A chapel was built in George Street and opened for worship in 1801. As Zion chapel was commonly called Bruce's chapel, so Salem chapel was spoken of as Rayson's chapel. In January 1935, Salem chapel was closed, the building and school were sold to the Wakefield Corporation for £1,000. The Ministers who have served this chapel, Benjamin Rayson, 1800–17 ; John Jefferson, 1819–22; Dr Cope, 1823–29; John Kelly, 1829–42; W. Lumb, 1842–48; W. Cread, 1848–52; W. Eastmead, 1852–83; W. Elstub, 1883–87; D. D. Waters, 1892–1911; W. E. Evans, 1915–20; F. T. Weekes, 1923–24; H. Sharp, 1931–32; H. Burn, 1933–35.

Salem Chapel Sunday School, *c.* 1930
Alongside Salem Chapel, stood the handsome premises of the Sunday school. It was set back from George Street and partially obscured by housing which stood betwixt the building and George Street.

The Baptists

Salem chapel was founded by a group of church members who were unhappy with church governance. The origin of the Primitive Methodist cause in Wakefield lies not with dissatisfaction of then-current Wesleyan or Methodist New Connexion ideals but with a schism from an Independent Chapel. In 1822, a difference of opinion over theology, Arminism as opposed to Calvanism, resulted in a congregation breaking away from the Independent movement, and establishing themselves as an Independent church body, under the leadership of the pastor, the Revd Dr Cope LLD.

The same year the small society purchased a plot of land in Quebec Street and employed Mr John Stead as Architect of their new chapel. It was a brick building, approximately fourteen yards square and was fitted up internally with pews and a gallery to seat 1,000 persons.

The building cost £1,000 to build and was opened on the 30 November 1823 by the Revd J. Farrar of Halifax at 10:30 a.m.

However, by 1836, the society was experiencing financial difficulties and had given up the Quebec Street Chapel, and it fell into the hands of the mortgager. Quebec Street Chapel opened as Wakefield Baptist chapel opened on 24 April 1836, the first minister, Mr Joseph Harvey, being appointed in May 1837. Dr Cope's congregation built a new chapel on Market Street, Wakefield, the foundation stone being laid in 1838. This chapel was enlarged in 1881 and closed in 1954.

The first baptismal service was held at Ossett on 9 January 1838 – there being no baptistry in the old independent chapel – and on 1st February 1838, the eight persons who were baptised, together with six others who were or who had been members of Baptist churches in other towns, agreed to unite themselves. It was the formation of this church of fourteen persons that led to the establishment of the Baptist denomination in Wakefield.

The members having increased to twenty-seven, the Church was formally constituted on 15 March 1839, and three deacons appointed. Mr Fox remained for four and a half years, adding seventy-three members to the Church. The necessity of a new chapel being imperative, land was secured and the present chapel opened on 20 March 1844, the Church then numbering ninety-nine members.

The first stone of the present building in Fair Ground Road was laid on 24 July 1843, by the Revd Peter Scott, Pastor of the Baptist Church, Shipley. The church at this time numbered ninety-nine members. The new chapel was opened on Wednesday, 20 March 1844. At the public breakfast next morning at West Parade Schoolroom the sum of £200 was promised towards the cost.

The building evidently taxed the resources of the people very severely, and the swift succession of brief pastorates suggests the difficulty the church had in supporting a settled ministry. During Mr Turner's pastorate the chapel was considerably improved, additional rooms built, an organ installed, and a hundred members were added to the Church. During the pastorate of Mr Ford (1882–93) the interior of the building was modernised, and following the First World War, electric light was installed through the generosity of one of the members.

Market Street Primitive Methodist Chapel
Opened in 1838, this building house the breakaway congregation from Salem Chapel, who had first met in a chapel on Quebec Street.

During the 1920s, members of the congregation felt that the chapel was in unsuitable surroundings, the buildings were sold, and land was purchased at Belle Isle for the erection of a new chapel, the stone laying ceremony for which took place on 10 June 1939. In addition to a chapel, the new buildings will provide a school and classrooms to be constructed from brickwork with flat roofs at a cost of £4,300.

The Baptist Chapel on Fairground Road, *c.* 1880
Built in the 1840s on Fair Ground road, the chapel stood hard two public houses, a malt kiln, hotel and the Cattle Market.

Holy Trinity Parish Chruch

One would hardly believe that a fine early Victorian church once stood where thus carpark and industrial units stands today. Holy Trinity church was closed in 1954 and demolished very soon after. The site was empty for many years, before being redeveloped. Today the only trace of their ever being a church here is in the street name Trinity Church Gate which ran to the southern edge of the church yard off Thornhill Street.

The apparent lack of religious belief (or at least its practice) among the working class and urban poor was a constant Victorian concern. The view that the absence from worship lead to the growth of anti-establishment activities, particularly Chartism was held in the 1830s and 1840s. These activities were impart to improve the lot of the working class, which is not surprising given their living conditions. Residents of nearby South Parade led the move to build a new church close to the fashionable development of South Parade. A meeting was held on 11 April 1838 at the Rolls Office, Manor House Yard, Kirkgate to discuss the building of a new church. The meeting was attended by the Revd D. Robinson, the Revd. W. Dawson, Robert Hodgson, Richard Dunn and Henry Lumb. The meeting agreed that '*the church shall be built upon part of a garden and croft respectively belonging to Robert Hodgson Esq and Samuel Holdsworth Esq, situate on the south side of and communicating with, George Street*'.

Eastern side of Holy Trinity Church, *c.* 1880
The church was built in a curious mix of gothic and classical architecture, then common in the 1830s. It was flanked by a small garden used for church activities. The church had rooms on the corner of George Street and West Parade, which were latterly the Trades and Labour Club before being demolished in the 1970s.

Interior of Holy Trinity Church, *c.* 1880
The interior of the church was in a simple gothic style. The chancel was enlivened by frescoes depicting the Ten Commandments and the Lord's Prayer. The large opening off the chancel was designed as an organ chamber, but the organ remained on the gallery under the tower.

Two months later, an advert was placed into the Leeds *Mercury* newspaper and the *West Riding Herald*, it read:

> To architects ... Wanted, plans and specifications for a new church at Wakefield to contain 1,000 sittings, one third to be free. For particulars apply to Mr Dawson Hon., Sec., Southgate, Wakefield. All plans to be delivered on or before 1st July next. Ten pounds ten shillings will be given for the plans and specifications approved by the committee.

The new church was to be in the gothic style and seat 600 persons in the body of the church and 400 in the galleries. The committee, headed by the Mr Dawson the Honorary Secretary, noted that the building was to cost no more than £2,500. Three plans were received by the committee and were copied into the minute book. The plans prepared by a Mr Billington were accepted. The bishop of Ripon, there being no bishop of Wakefield until 1888, was asked to lay the foundation stones. The church was opened in 1839, but not until 10 October 1844 did it become a Parish Church. A chancel was added sometime later. The church was attended by members of the Dykes family. Frederick Dykes was

North Façade of Holy Trinity
Church, 1943
Holy Trinity church showing
the principal façade on George
Street. The building was
demolished in 1954.

manager of a Wakefield bank and resided latterly at No. 4 South Parade. His brother was
the great hymn tune writer John Bachus Dykes. The church closed in 1954.

4. Dance Hall, Town Hall and Organ Building Factory

In Crown Court, the building displaying 'Town Hall' on its façade has a fascinating story. It had originally been built as the 'New Assembly Rooms'. The George and Crown Yard, leading from Crown Court, was named after an inn that once stood at the Silver Street end and was an early home of the Freemasons. Like many hundreds of buildings in Wakefield, the New Assembly Rooms building purpose changed over its 200-year history and is still doing so. As often happens, a building's use often changes from those of the original builders. The Old Town Hall in Crown Court certainly has changed in purpose over its 200-year history.

The building was erected in 1798 as new assembly rooms, the original assembly rooms being a part of the White Hart Inn which stood on Kirkgate. It was variously known as the New Assembly Rooms or the Music Hall. Wakefield's first newspaper, *The Wakefield Star*, which was founded in 1803 was published from here. The New Assembly rooms as a dance hall and music venue seems to have closed in 1821 or 1822, perhaps due to the building of the Music Saloon nearby on the recently laid out Wood Street.

Wood Street is not one of Wakefield's ancient medieval streets. The area now occupied by Wood Street was before 1806 open ground beyond Rishworth Street. In that year 1806, the Rev William Wood sold some of the land to the West Riding Magistrates on which was built the County Court House; the land opposite the site of the Court House was formerly a stone quarry which was also sold, and the remaining land was laid out as Wood Street.

Wood Street, *c.* 1900
Looking up Wood Street around 1900 towards
St Johns. Parts of the street today remain little
changed today compared to the view of around 1880.

On this street were built some of the major civic buildings of the town. In 1820, subscriptions were raised to build public rooms at the town-centre end of the street, with a grand Music Saloon on the upper floor. Shares were offered at £25. Prominent among its promoters was the Vicar of Wakefield, Samuel Sharp. It seems that money was slow to come in. The building work took many months and the saloon itself did not open until 22 December 1823.

Methodists of the New Connexion are first recorded in Wakefield by 1800, being a splinter group from West Parade Wesleyan church. In 1822 saw the first chapel being opened, when they moved from their rented room in Garden Street. The New Assembly Rooms were opened as a chapel for the Methodist New Connexion on 24 March by the Revd Garbutt of Leeds at ten o'clock. The Revd Roberts of Huddersfield preached at 2:00 p.m. in the afternoon, and the Revd Wood of Dewsbury preached in the evening

The Music Saloon
The Music Saloon was erected in 1823. Here we see it in a view of around 1880. It housed the Wakefield Mechanics Institution from 1842 until 1935.

at 6:30 p.m. Collections were taken at all the services to cover the expense of the fittings.

This first chapel was administered by the Leeds New Connexion circuit but was later transferred to Barnsley. The congregation moved to new premises in 1858 when the premises were destroyed by fire. The congregation moved to a room in Kirkgate which had once been a casino hall, which was rented to the society for the annual sum of £14 by the Fernades brothers. The room was set out with pews which were rented to the members, raising £1 3s 9d in 1865 and a year later £2 6s 10d.

Despite humble origins, meeting in rented rooms, the society flourished and was able to open its first purpose built chapel on Grove Road in 1866. It closed in 1978.

Kirkgate c. 1880
Kirkgate around 1880. Little changed since the 1860s, it was somewhere here in a former Casino that Methodists met to worship.

Returning once more to the story of the New Assembly Rooms, from 1841, the building was used by the then newly formed Mechanics Institute but removed to the Music Saloon in June 1842, premises it would purchase in 1855. A second educational body between 1845 and 1858 the Wakefield Church Institution used a part of the building for its library, lectures and evening classes.

On 24 November 1845, the Revd T. B. Parkinson, incumbent of St Mary's carish church Primrose Hill, organised a meeting to consider the formation of a Church Institution, its objects being to advance the principles of the Church of England, the promotion of general knowledge in subordination to religion, the cultivation of church music and the encouragement of friendly intercourse among all classes of churchmen. In 1858, the Institution moved to rented premises in Queen Street and then a room in the Mechanics Institute and then a shop in Wood Street. Purpose built premises were erected in 1863.

St Mary's Parish Church
The new parish church was consecrated 29 August 1854 by the bishop of Ripon. The building alongside the church, the Parish School, was opened on 11 May 1857.

Interior of St Mary's Parish Church
St Mary's parish church, Primrose Hill. The
parish was formed in 1844. The church was
fitted out as cheaply as possible, the windows
were plain glass, and of the proposed peel of
eight bells, only one could be afforded. An
organ chamber was added in 1886 and stained
glass memorial windows erected in the
chancel. The church was closed in 1966 and
was demolished soon after.

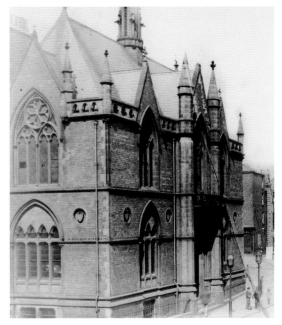

The Church Institute, *c.* 1880
In 1862, the site of the Medieval manor
bake house was bought for £735 and
Mr A. B. Highman prepared plans for the
new building. The new hall cost £2,350 to
build and provided a library, news room and
lecture hall. For some year's, the Institution
was very successful, providing weekly lectures
to its members on science, art or literature as
well as entertainments of a lighter character.
The building was closed and the Institution
wound up in May 1911. The building was
demolished in January 1964.

Wakefield Town Hall, *c.* 1880
The site between the Court
House and the Public Rooms
(formerly the City Museum,
now premsies for Wakefield
College) was purchased by
Wakefield Corporation in 1854,
but it was not until 1877 that the
building work commenced. It
was designed by T. W. Colcutt,
a London architect, in a
French Renaissance style. The
foundation stone was laid by
the Mayor, Alderman W. H. Gill,
solicitor, in October 1877, and the
building was opened in October
1880 by the Mayor, W. H. Lee,
worsted spinner.

In June 1858, the building was gutted by fire. It was this burnt out shell that Wakefield's councillors decided to lease as a Town Hall in 1861, paying the owner, John Bayldon, a substantial sum to rebuild it to the Corporation's needs. The site between the Court House and the Music Saloon on Wood Street (formerly the City Museum, now premises for Wakefield College) was purchased by Wakefield Corporation in 1854, but it was not until 1877 that the building work commenced on a new town hall. The building was designed by T. W. Colcutt, a London architect, in a French Renaissance style. The foundation stone was laid by the Mayor, Alderman W.H. Gill, solicitor, in October 1877, and the building was opened in October 1880 by the Mayor, W. H. Lee, whose names are commemorated by Gill Street and Lee Street which adjoin the building.

With Wakefield Council leaving the building, in 1893 the building was transformed into a factory to build pipe organs for the business of Alfred Kirkland. Alfred Kirkland was a native of Mansfield, and from 1873 he worked for the Wakefield organ builder Francis Booth, who had built pipes organs in Yorkshire, France and the West Indies. Francis Booth died in 1874, and the business was taken over by his son Henry.

Kirkland was foreman and manager for Henry Booth, until August 1875 when, it is thought, he bought out Henry Booth and set himself up as an organ builder, trading under the name 'Alfred Kirkland'.

Alfred Kirkland was a native of Mansfield born in 1852. The 1861 census lists him living with his father, Thomas, who by this date was a widower. Thomas was born in

Mansfield in 1822 and was an Engineer employing fourteen men and four boys. Living with the young Alfred, was his aunt Anna Kirkland, his father's sister, who was born in Mansfield in 1833. Alfred had a younger brother Thomas, who was born in 1854. The family was fairly affluent and could afford to employ two servants. Mary A Preston a native of Bulwell in Nottinghamshire, born in 1837 and Mary Rickett, from Hockerton, Nottinghamshire was born in 1840.

At age twelve, after leaving school he was apprenticed to F. W. Jardine of Manchester. Both Alfred and Thomas Kirkland are listed on the 1871 as being lodgers in Shelford, Barton upon Irwell, Lancashire. Alfred is listed as an organ builder and Thomas as a Mechanical Engineer. They were lodging with Thomas Preston and his wife Ann, and their daughter Sarah Preston and two nephews, Henry and William Entwistle. He then worked for Francis Booth from around 1873. Kirklands' first job as an independent organ builder was the installation of a two manual organ in St Matthews Anglican Parish Church, Lightcliffe, which was opened on 21st September 1875.[8] In January 1876, Kirkland was instructed to prepare a new organ for Batley Carr Parish Church.[9] In November 1876, Kirkland opened a new organ at Farsley Baptist Church with the case being made by Mr Atkinson of Leeds. [10]

By the time of his marriage to Kate Grinley in 1880, he had prospered sufficiently to move to a new house, 'Hardcastle' Mount Ville, off Sludge Lane, now Westfield Road. Here he employed a domestic servant, Alice Ford, who also looked after his infant daughter Annie, born in 1881. At this time, Kirkland employed fourteen men and five apprentices at 'The Factory' 181 Howard Street. By 1881, Kirkland realised that he would need to expand commercially into other towns and cities, if he was going to become a National builder. In 1882, Kirkland opened his first London branch at 14 Hanover Street, which was followed two years later with a branch at 5a Northampton Place. The London branches were far more important monetarily than Wakefield, so in 1887, he left Wakefield and moved to 57 Mercers Road, Islington. Here his young family would grow up. By the time of the move, a son Thomas J. had been born. Three more children followed in London, Edith M. in 1887, Alfred E. in 1890 and Walter in 1892. He employed two servants, Annie Simnett, twenty-one years, a nurse Elizabeth Scott, nineteen years, as a domestic servant. His servants in 1901 were Eveline Smith and Gerturde Lawrence. Thomas would later become headmaster of Kings School Ely and Canon of Ely Cathedral.

Kirkland between 1887 and 1893 had no Wakefield branch, and it appears Wakefield staff were laid off. This resulted in the founding of Marshall Brothers Ltd of Wakefield. Kirkland moved to 113 Cottenham Road, Upper Holloway, London North in June 1896 from 655a Upper Holloway, London. The premises comprised an office, erecting room, store room, workshop and strip of land, Kirkland only leased the premises.[11] He then moved to 155a Marlborough Road, Holloway in 1908, and remained here until 1923. A branch was opened at 22 Carrington Street Nottingham in 1891. This branch also

8   The *Leeds Mercury*, 21 September 1875.
9   The *Huddersfiield Chronicle and West Yorkshire Advertiser*, 1 January 1876.
10   The *Leeds Mercury*, 29 November 1876.
11   The *Standard*, 6 June 1896.

dealt with orders and tuning round for the North of England, as it was advertised as the Nottingham & Halifax Branch in 1982.

In order to expand the tuning and maintenance round, and also expand the company, the organ building concern of Bryceson Brothers was bought out in 1893. A fourth branch was opened on Duncombe Road, London in 1896. Alfred Kirkland was now a national organ builder of note.

The Duncombe Road and 113 Cottenham Road branches were merged in 1907, when new premises at 155A Marlborough Road Upper Holloway were purchased. A new Wakefield branch was opened in 1893 in the Old Town Hall, Crown Court. From 1904, Kirkland obtained all his pipes for Northern and Midland organs from 'Marshall Brothers Ltd' of Wakefield. The Wakefield branch moved in 1917 to City Chambers, 38 Wood Street, where it remained until closure in 1923, when Alfred Kirkland sold the concern to Norman & Beard Ltd. Kirkland died in 1929.

In the twentieth century the Old Town Hall was used as rented office space. Today it is now luxury apartments. The once lofty erecting hall of the organ building factory on the first floor which was open to the rafters is now 'loft apartments'.

8. Bibliography and Further Reading

William, Albert, *The Turnpike Road System, in England 1663-1840* (Cambridge: Cambridge University Press, 1972).

Banks, W. S., *Walks about Wakefield* (Wakefield: Wakefield Historical Publications, 1987).

Camidge, C. E., *A History of Wakefield and its Industrial and Fine Art Exhibition* (Wakefield, 1866).

Clarkson, Henry, *Memories of Merry Wakefield* (Wakefield: Wakefield Historical Publications).

Dawson, Paul Lindsay, *Booth of Wakefield Organ Builders to the World* (Wakefield: ABGI, 2011).

Goodchild, John, *Aspects of Medieval Wakefield and its Legacy* (Wakefield: Wakefield Historical Publications).

Goodchild, John, *The Coal Kings of Yorkshire* (Wakefield Historical Publications).

John FSA, James, *History of Worsted Manufacture in England* (London: Longman, Broom, Longmans and Roberts, 1857).

Priestley, Joseph, *Historical Account of the Navigable Rivers, Canals and Railways of Great Britain.* (Wakefield: Nicholson, 1831).

Taylor, Kate, *The Making of Wakefield: 1801-1900* (Barnsley, Wharncliffe, 2008).

Taylor, Kate (ed.), *Wakefield and District Heritage*, 2 vols (Wakefield: Wakefield EAHY Committee).

Walker, J. W., *Wakefield its History and its People*, 2 vols (Wakefield: Private, 1936).

Wilson, Richard George, *Gentleman Merchants: The Merchant Community in Leeds, 1700–1830.* (Manchester: Manchester University Press, 1971).

Acknowledgements

In the preparation of this, I must single out for the support, guidance, encouragement as well as most generous provision of research material, editorial oversight and photographs my friend the late Kate Taylor MA (Oxon) who passed away on 5 May 2015. This book is based upon five lectures given in Wakefield in the past couple of years by myself and published here for the first time to make these little known aspects of Wakefield known to a larger audience.